COVENANT • BIBLE • STUDIES

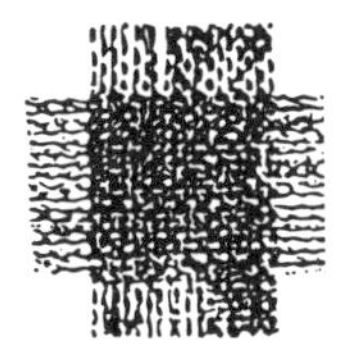

Paul's Prison Letters

LaTaunya Bynum

faithQuest® ✦ Brethren Press®

Unless otherwise noted, scripture quotations are from the New Revised Standard Version of the Bible, copyrighted 1989 by the Division of Christian Education of the National Council of the Churches of Christ in the U.S.A.

Cover photo by Vista III Design, Inc., Bloomington, MN 55439

00 99 98 97 96   5 4 3 2 1

Library of Congress Catalog Card Number: 96-84214

Manufactured in the United States of America

Contents

Foreword

The Covenant Bible Study Series was first developed for a denominational program in the Church of the Brethren and the Christian Church (Disciples of Christ). This program, called People of the Covenant, was founded on the concept of relational Bible study and has been adopted by several other denominations and small groups who want to study the Bible in a community rather than alone.

Relational Bible study is marked by certain characteristics, some of which differ from other types of Bible study. For one, it is intended for small groups of people who can meet face-to-face on a regular basis and share frankly with an intimate group.

It is important to remember that relational Bible study is anchored in covenantal history. God covenanted with people in Old Testament history, established a new covenant in Jesus Christ, and covenants with the church today.

Relational Bible study takes seriously a corporate faith. As each person contributes to study, prayer, and work, the group becomes the real body of Christ. Each one's contribution is needed and important. "For just as the body is one and has many members, and all the members of the body, though many, are one body, so it is with Christ. . . . Now you are the body of Christ and individually members of it" (1 Cor. 12:12,17).

Relational Bible study helps both individuals and the group to claim the promise of the Spirit and the working of the Spirit. As one person testified, "In our commitment to one another and in our sharing, something happened. . . . We were woven together in love by the master Weaver. It is something that can happen only when two or three or seven are gathered in God's name, and we know the promise of God's presence in our lives."

The symbol of these covenant Bible study groups is the burlap cross. The interwoven threads, the uniqueness of each strand, the unrefined fabric, and the rough texture characterize covenant groups. The people in the groups are unique but interrelated; they are imperfect and unpolished, but loving and supportive.

The shape that these divergent threads create is the cross, the symbol for all Christians of the resurrection and presence with us of Christ our Savior. Like the burlap cross, we are brought together, simple and ordinary, to be sent out again in all directions to be in the world.

For people who choose to use this study in a small group, the following guidelines will help create an atmosphere in which support will grow and faith will deepen.

1. As a small group of learners, we gather around God's word to discern its meaning for today.
2. The words, stories, and admonitions we find in scripture come alive for today, challenging and renewing us.
3. All people are learners and all are leaders.
4. Each person will contribute to the study, sharing the meaning found in the scripture and helping to bring meaning to others.
5. We recognize each other's vulnerability as we share out of our own experience, and in sharing we learn to trust others and to be trustworthy.

Additional suggestions for study and group-building are provided in the "Sharing and Prayer" section. They are intended for use in the hour preceding the Bible study to foster intimacy in the covenant group and relate personal sharing to the Bible study topic.

Welcome to this study. As you search the scriptures, may you also search yourself. May God's voice and guidance and the love and encouragement of brothers and sisters in Christ challenge you to live more fully the abundant life God promises.

Preface

Letters of encouragement and other greetings from friends mean so much to us. Whether we are far from home, going through difficult transitions in life, or simply feeling alone and discouraged, personal contacts that say "I care" keep us going during the tough times.

This became evident to me several years ago as my mother struggled with Alzheimer's Disease. Her last year had been long and stressful. It was a difficult time for the family, as we learned how to cope with the strokes that deprived our mother of speech and finally led to her death just after Thanksgiving. How special were the expressions of love and concern offered by friends—in person, in telephone calls, and in letters! From across the miles flowed loving encouragement and support. I experienced renewed faith, joy, and hope.

Consider the inestimable value of friends—friends who are there for us in times of grief and pain, discouragement and change; friends who keep making contact, in spite of the miles or their own trying circumstances; friends who share faith and help us live in hope; friends who call us to a deeper knowledge of Jesus Christ; friends who help us experience God's presence in all of life.

We need such friends. We need friends like the Apostle Paul, who wrote very personal letters to his Christian brother Philemon and to the young churches in Philippi and Colossae. Paul's warm greetings, his expressions of gratitude and thanksgiving, his words of hope and encouragement, his calls to faithful living, along with the blessings that close his letters—all are expressions of Paul's friendship and caring. In spite of his own circumstances, in spite of being held prisoner, Paul wrote of hope and joy.

This study of Paul's prison letters calls us to a new appreciation of friends and challenges us to become more faithful friends. It offers us ancient affirmations of faith and calls us to make our own affirmations about Jesus Christ. It shows us the servant way of life Jesus chose and calls us to freedom in Christ as we choose a servant lifestyle.

As you study these letters from a good friend, Paul, may you find joy and hope, freedom and new life among Christian friends.

—June Adams Gibble, Coordinator
People of the Covenant

Recommended Resources

Achtemeier, Paul, ed. *Harper's Dictionary of the Bible.* Harper and Row, 1985.

Craddock, Fred B. *Philippians* (Interpretation Series). John Knox Press, 1985.

Martin, Ernest D. *Colossians and Philemon* (Believers Church Bible Commentary). Herald Press, 1993.

Martin, Ralph. *Ephesians, Colossians, Philemon* (Interpretation Series). John Knox Press, 1991.

1

Persisting, Though Opposed

Philippians 1

Writing during confinement to congregations at Philippi and Colossae and to his friend Philemon, Paul urged the recipients of his letters to stand strong in their faith in Jesus Christ. Their faith in Christ would enable them to do what was right even in the most trying circumstances. The gospel message would abound.

Personal Preparation

1. To gain historical background and insight into the founding of the church at Philippi, read Acts 16:11ff.
2. Read Philippians 1. As you read, what questions are raised in your mind? Jot questions on paper and plan to bring them to your group meeting.
3. Recall a time you experienced strong opposition. How was your faith helpful as you faced your opponent? How did you handle fear or discouragement in that situation?
4. Ponder Paul's statement in Philippians 1:18—that he rejoices in the midst of opposition. How could he say that? Are you able to do it?

Understanding

A woman long retired from missionary service in Latin America recalled being held under house arrest in a small town caught in the crossfire between government soldiers and guerrilla forces. One of the days of her confinement happened to be Easter Sunday. There in her house she pondered the meaning of the resurrection for a person who could not come and go as she wished. *How will I celebrate this Easter when I cannot even go to church?* she wondered. She decided to read all four gospel accounts of the resurrection of Christ, she sang her favorite Easter hymns, and for lunch that day she ate bread and grapes.

Any form of isolation or captivity gives us time to reflect on what is important. For the imprisoned missionary, it was the meaning of Easter. For the Apostle Paul, whether he was in jail or out, it was his absolute trust in the risen Christ. He could apparently view any form of opposition as another part of the plan by which the gospel would advance.

Prison Is Part of the Plan

Detention served to reaffirm Paul's call to ministry and his faith in God's wise workings. It is not entirely clear why Paul was imprisoned, however, nor do we know exactly in what conditions he was held. Was he in a cave, a house, or a military barracks? We do know he had access to visitors, gifts, and mail, and that those kinds of privileges were reserved for prisoners of a higher status, dwelling in a more relaxed setting. On the other hand, Paul often referred to himself as a man in chains. He mentioned the imperial guard, so it is likely that he was kept under some kind of military detention in one of the imperial cities. Agreeing with the traditional view, we assume he was held in Rome, although he may have been at Ephesus or Caesarea.

In any case, Paul had not yet come to trial, and it was in the context of having been arraigned but not yet tried that Paul wrote certain letters. Many believe he wrote two sets of letters from Roman imprisonment: the four Prison Epistles (Ephesians, Philippians, Colossians, and Philemon) and the three Pastoral Epistles (1 and 2 Timothy and Titus). In our present unit of study, we will look at three of the Prison Epistles, starting with Philippians.

Paul loved the Philippian Christians deeply, so this is the most personal and revealing of all his letters to churches. He used the first-person singular over fifty times in addressing his flock. Paul founded the church of Philippi with the conversion of Lydia (see Acts 16:11-15), and his affection for the people is evident in the tenderness of his greeting and in his thanksgiving for them. This congregation occupied Paul's mind and heart in the way our home congregations can exert strong emotional pulls on us, even if we live far away and are unable to attend regularly. Surely the church in Philippi was memorable to the apostle, with its membership including a converted businesswoman, a former demonic soothsayer, a jailer, and perhaps numerous prisoners. What a diverse church!

Paul raised two major concerns as he wrote to the Philippians in chapter 1. First, he wanted his brothers and sisters to know that God would finish the good work of salvation and fellowship that had begun in them. Second, he wanted them to understand how the cause of the gospel was being served even by his imprisonment.

The Good Work Will Continue

Paul wrote words of joy and encouragement throughout the book of Philippians. In 1:6 he wrote that "the one who began a good work among you will bring it to completion by the day of Jesus Christ." He shared his confidence that in the day of Christ, all of the Philippians would know a twofold blessing: they would have grown in maturity, and the fruit of their labor would bring glory to God (1:9-11).

Do such words indicate from the outset of the book that Paul knew about a conflict among the Philippians? We may find here an implicit reference to tension in the community, because Paul seemed to go out of his way to say in verse 4 that he was praying for all of the members of the church. Later, in chapter 4, a problem between two of the women would be revealed. The implied problem is one every pastor encounters as she or he navigates the waters between authority and intimacy with a congregation.

I remember when a pastor and his wife developed a close friendship with another couple in the church. The two couples ate dinner together at least once a week. They vacationed together. Their children were best friends. The two families were so close that the line between pastor and parishioner was erased. The pastor began to confide in his friend about confidential church matters.

Other members of the congregation resented the obvious intimacy between the two families. The situation became so tense that the minister had to pray and work hard to repair the damage. He had become too involved with one family, to the neglect of several other families in the church.

Church leaders do need to be close to their members. Too much closeness, however, can blur a needed objectivity for the pastor and people. It may be that some in the Philippian church believed that Paul was closer to certain members than he was to others. Paul assured them that each of them shared in the ministry with him. In spite of struggles with disunity in the fellowship, God's work would be carried to fruition.

Opposition Cannot Stop It

Disharmony in the church cannot thwart the work of the gospel, nor can opposition from outside the church. His experience of imprisonment was Paul's second reason for writing. For Paul, being detained was an occasion to proclaim Jesus with joy. He was not weakened by the experience, nor was he threatened by the envious rival preachers who only began their work after he was arrested. What mattered to him was that the gospel was preached and the guards and other prisoners received the benefit. Paul knew that the power of the gospel does not depend on the messenger's motives. He also knew that it was not possible to "unhear" the gospel, no matter what attitude the hearer held at the time.

Paul wanted to do more than just inform the Philippians that he was doing well, even in confinement. He wanted the Philippians to do well, too. He offered them words of explanation about his trial, hoping that their anxiety for him would subside. Any of us who has ever watched a friend or loved one suffer knows the need for such an explanation. We want to know: *What does it all mean?*

Paul's answer was that his imprisonment meant, "Christ is proclaimed in every way." Paul responded to opposition with tremendous faith in God, and God's purposes were therefore unfolding. The boldness with which the gospel was proclaimed stood in stark contrast to the fear that once overwhelmed the disciples immediately following the arrest of Jesus. Paul's arrest brought no hiding and no denial from his followers. In fact, the brothers and sisters now preached with even greater confidence.

Paul's words of explanation challenge the church today as it tries to make sense of the violence and abuse plaguing Christians around the world. What makes all the difference is the work of the Spirit in us and among us, as Paul affirmed in verse 19. As Bible commentator Fred Craddock says, "Only by the presence of the Holy Spirit can the church experience the miraculous shift of attitude from assuming that wherever the Lord is there is no suffering, to believing that wherever there is suffering, there the Lord is."

Difficult situations will come, but despair need not rest in our hearts. Jobs will be lost, relationships will crumble, opponents will do their best to undermine our efforts. It is in these times that faith helps us to stand "firm in one spirit" (1:27).

Discussion and Action

1. Share some of the questions that came to mind during your reading of Philippians 1 (see Personal Preparation question 2).
2. Tell about a circumstance that caused you to suffer for your faith. How would you evaluate your response, in light of the way Paul responded to his imprisonment? What might you do differently in a similar situation in the future?
3. Paul was filled with faith in Christ, but he was also a man in crisis. In fact, some scholars think that when Paul said, "My desire is to depart and be with Christ," he might have been depressed, perhaps even considering suicide. What do you think? In your opinion, how should Christians deal with depression?
4. Paul said, "For to me, living is Christ" (1:21). From what you know of Paul, how did his actions confirm this statement? In what practical ways could the statement be evident in the life of a present-day believer? How is it true in your life?
5. Tell about a time you saw the power of the gospel at work in the midst of opposition. Drawing on your own experience, what advice about being ready for the tough times would you give to a new Christian?
6. Nathan McCall and Patrice Gaines are reporters for *The Washington Post.* In their younger years, each spent time in jail for criminal conduct. Imprisonment was a defining moment for each of them, and both have written that jail helped them recognize the need to change. When have you been forced to come to terms with self-destructive behavior? When have you had to make hard decisions about the direction you wanted the rest of your life to take? Did a period of solitude or isolation help you in this process? Explain.
7. What is your attitude to people in jail—whether they are guilty or not?
8. Think as a group about a form of opposition your congregation is facing. Does this opposition demonstrate that you are obeying God? How is Christ proclaimed in the midst of this opposition?

2

Having the Mind of Christ
Philippians 2—3:1

Living together as joyful Christians requires wisdom and diligence because harmonious relationships must be cultivated. Paul urged the Philippians to have the mind of Christ as they continued to form a community. In this way they would be able to treat one another with respect, resolve their conflicts, and work out their salvation through fruitful service.

Personal Preparation

1. Read through Philippians 2—3:1 and write down some words and phrases that seem important.
2. Make a list of people you consider to be Christian servants, people who seem to have Christlike attitudes and actions. What, in your opinion, identifies these people as servants of Christ?
3. Spend some time considering this question: Can people in the church disagree about their faith and beliefs and still share the mind of Christ? How would you explain your response to a person who is considering joining your church? Try using an example of a recent conflict faced by your congregation.

Understanding

During World War II, a priest operated an orphanage in Poland. One day Nazi soldiers approached him saying they had come to take the children to a safe place in Russia. The priest knew the Nazis were lying to him, and he insisted on traveling with the children on the long train ride to the death camp. If the children were going to be "safe," he would be "safe" with them.

For that priest, to be a Christian was to live and die with the ones who were in his care. In my country, to be a Christian is rarely a life-threatening commitment. Paul wrote that to be a Christian is to "look not to your own interests, but to the interests of others" (2:4). For most of us the application of the call to be Christian takes place in decidedly mundane circumstances. Who will I encourage—or avoid—at the potluck dinner tonight? Do we really have to change the order of worship just to please the choir members? Why is the commission using our funds in *that* way? Having the mind of Christ has global, life-or-death implications, but it certainly has everyday, practical applications as well.

How do we *be Christian?* Paul suggested that it has to do with the attitudes we choose, especially in the midst of conflict.

Regarding Others with Humility

Apparently there was a specific conflict at Philippi. Tension filled the community, and 2:1-4, 14, and 3:1 contain language that a mediator might use in trying to diffuse a sticky situation.

In Philippi, putting others first would be an exercise in humility and obedience to God. It did not mean that all church members had to agree on every detail of their life together. Philippi was, after all, a human community. Such agreement simply is not possible, then or now. Paul's concern had to do with working out healthy ways to resolve disagreement in the Christian community.

Was the Philippian community about to come apart? We cannot say. What we can do is recall instances of conflict in our own congregations and then reflect on how those tensions were resolved in either helpful or harmful ways. There is still much that threatens to fragment the church. Some conflicts that on the surface do not seem important can put congregations at risk. A serious argument about what color carpet to put in the sanctuary likely masks a deeper issue of control and resistance to change, for example. Then there are tense church council meetings about whether to add a drum and electric guitar to the musical ensemble. The heated exchanges probably have less to do with musical tastes than with expectations that several different generations bring to worship on Sunday morning.

One of the myths of church life is that it is conflict-free. We have this perception that Christians seldom disagree and that when they do it is of little importance, so church conflicts tend to leave us angry and confused. How can we disagree and not put our faith at risk?

Handling Conflicts with Christ's Attitude

Whatever the source of the tension in Philippi, Paul called the members to disagree without being disagreeable. He gave them several ways to address the tension. He told them, for example, that they should have the same purposes and goals in mind for the spread of the kingdom, they should love one another, they should remember that they are partners in the gospel with him and with each other, and they must "do nothing from selfish ambition or conceit" (2:3).

Do *nothing* from self-interest? How is that possible? Are we not all governed by self-interest to a large extent? Surely Paul would support our having a healthy self-interest in, say, becoming faithful followers of the Lord Jesus Christ. The self-interest Paul denounced is the kind that puts oneself first *with no regard for others.* He addressed the destructiveness that comes when we never seek to discover what our brothers and sisters in the community need and want. In any age, whether in Paul's day or our own, these hymn-words ought to describe the essence of our relationships with other people:

> Will you let me be your servant,
> let me be as Christ to you?
> Pray that I may have the grace
> to let you be my servant, too.
>
> We are pilgrims on a journey,
> we are trav'lers on the road.
> We are here to help each other
> walk the mile and bear the load.

All of these instructions from Paul are built upon a crucial, foundational premise: that we are constantly looking to Jesus as our primary example of caring for others first. "Let the same mind be in you that was in Christ Jesus," Paul said in 2:5. To have the mind of Christ is to understand that Christ was raised up and exalted in part because he was able to do two things most of us find incredibly difficult: Jesus humbled himself, and Jesus was totally obedient to God. We are used to thinking of ourselves as independent, free-thinking adults. We are able and determined to make our own decisions and find our own ways. Obedience and humility just do not fit. To us, obedience and humility seem demeaning.

What would it require to take the first small step toward humility? Perhaps it would mean choosing a new attitude to the next person who walks into the room—recognizing that *what they are for us* is largely a matter of *what we have become for them.* Consider this anonymous saying that holds much wisdom: "Our attitude toward the world around us depends upon what we are ourselves. If we are selfish, we will be suspicious of others. If we are of a generous nature, we will be likely to be more trustful. If we are quite honest with ourselves, we won't always be anticipating deceit in others. In a sense, looking at the people around you is like looking in a mirror."

Our passage from Philippians points us away from ourselves, encourages us not only to look in the mirror of others' faces but also to *keep looking at Jesus* even in the most practical and mundane situations of life. Jesus was not demeaned by obedience or humility; in fact, he chose to live in humility and obedience. We are tempted to look at 2:5-11 and see a kind of mechanical transaction. That is, we too quickly correlate humility on earth and reward in heaven. To yield to that temptation is to miss the point. Jesus chose servanthood for the purpose of obedience alone. And he is our supreme example.

Working It Out with Service

Paul urged the recipients of his letter to work out their own salvation. They had to do this because, while Paul loved them and wanted what was best for them, they were ultimately responsible for developing their own relationships with God. It was a matter of recognizing what was already there. God had already begun to work in them, so it would be up to them to find ways to demonstrate that their relationship with the Lord was a fruitful one.

Paul offered two of their contemporaries as examples of fruitful discipleship. He pointed to Timothy and Epaphroditus, his "son" and "brother" in the faith respectively. Both men had served Paul well, and he trusted them enough to commend them to the church at Philippi as role models of servanthood.

Timothy was an early Christian convert and had been with Paul for a long time. Epaphroditus was known to the Philippians and had put his own health at risk to be with Paul, helping him on their behalf. Paul continued in his plan to come to Philippi, but in the meantime he was confident enough in the gifts of these men, for whom he had been a spiritual mentor, that he would send them in his place. Here again we catch Paul's deep love for these people.

Paul's final words in this section are of advice that will serve the church well when tensions threaten to overwhelm it: "Rejoice in the LORD!" One man who was able to blend rejoicing with a firm commitment to church unity was Dan West, founder of Heifer Project International. Very active at the local church level, Dan often spoke forcefully at church council meetings about his convictions. On one occasion, he failed to convince other church members about a particular matter he believed in deeply. After he was outvoted, he reminded others about how important it is to put the body of Christ first. He announced that he would support the others' viewpoint with just as much enthusiasm as he had formerly supported his own.

Our true unity shines through our common worship. Unity is based not upon mere consensus, not even upon humble submission. Ultimately, we are eternally yoked by the most powerful of all bonds: we are "sharing in the Spirit" (2:1).

Discussion and Action

1. Together review the lists you developed in response to question 2 in Personal Preparation. Share your insights about people you have observed displaying Christlike attitudes.
2. Focus on 2:2-5 to review Paul's list of ways to address tension in the Philippian congregation. How do his instructions compare with reconciliation steps that are used in churches today? What might you add in order to make the scriptural list more complete and practical for use in your own church?
3. Refer to the opening story about the self-sacrificial priest. When have you *chosen* to suffer on behalf of someone else? In what practical ways can North American Christians apply the principle of self-sacrifice today? What might self-sacrifice look like in your own community, family, or church? Can you give some examples?
4. Philippians 2:5-11 is known as a "Christ hymn." Imagine it being used as part of a worship service—in ancient times, or today. Name some possible sermon titles that might also be a part of the service.
5. How would you define the term *servant* in relation to Christian servanthood? When have you been a servant? When was someone a servant to you?
6. How do we disagree as Christians, while still sharing the same mind? If possible, raise an issue of disagreement in your covenant group. Brainstorm some possible approaches

to resolving the conflict. How does this passage in Philippians guide your thinking?

7. Focus on the following quote from this session: "In a sense, looking at the people around you is like looking in a mirror." To what extent do you agree or disagree with this statement? Share a personal example that supports your point of view.

3

A Warning . . . and a Prize

Philippians 3:2—4:1

Paul warned the Philippians about spiritual threats coming from groups that placed their faith in works-righteousness. Though he, too, could boast of a flawless spiritual heritage and tremendous religious accomplishments, such things no longer impressed him. His eyes were on the prize: heavenly citizenship and its promise of resurrection and transformation. That is where our eyes, too, should focus, for "it is from there that we are expecting a Savior" (3:20).

Personal Preparation

1. As you read through Philippians 3:2—4:1, notice Paul's harsh language describing people who are disturbing the church's peace. Does this language bother you? If so, think about what alternative language you might use.
2. Paul listed several reasons for confidence as he considered his spiritual gifts. What are your reasons for confidence in life? What are your spiritual gifts?
3. Take a moment to list your five greatest accomplishments on a sheet of paper. Now consider which of these you would give up for the sake of the gospel. What would giving up that accomplishment mean to you, in practical terms? Why would it be difficult or easy to give up?
4. Reread 3:10 and 12. How do you "know Christ" in your life?

Understanding

Sometimes a few stern words of warning from a friend can be just the thing we need to get us back on the right track. In hindsight, at least, we can sometimes admit that. Perhaps young pastor Trembath eventually came to that point of acceptance after receiving this letter from John Wesley in 1775:

> *To Mr. John Trembath, Tiverton, September 21—*
>
> The plain reason why I did not design to speak with you at Launceston was that I had no hope of doing you good. I observed long ago that you are not patient of reproof; and I fear you are less so now than ever. But since you desire it, I will tell you once more what I think concerning you.
>
> I think you tasted of the powers of the world to come thirteen or fourteen years ago and were then simple of heart and willing to spend and be spent for Christ. But not long after, not being sufficiently on your guard, you suffered loss by being applauded. This revived and increased your natural vanity, which was the harder to be checked because of your innate stubbornness.
>
> O remember from whence you have fallen! Repent and do the first works! First, recover the life of God in your own soul and walk as Christ walked. Walk with God as you did twelve years ago. Then you might again be useful to His children.

Here is an invitation for someone to break with the past and move into the new. Although candid warnings can hurt, usually they are offered in the hope of doing good. That was the Apostle Paul's purpose, as well, when he wrote to the Philippian believers to be careful. Notice the unmistakable mood shift between the joyful and gentle advice given to these same people in chapters 1 and 2, and the warning sounded at the beginning of chapter 3: *Beware! . . . Beware! . . . Beware!*

A Triple Threat

The Philippians needed a warning because Paul saw that their faith was being threatened. What was the source of the threat? The possibilities emerge in 3:2. Whether Paul was using three epithets to designate one group, or whether there were actually three different groups is not clear. In any case, the terms themselves represent three kinds of threats. We might picture each as a dangerous tine on a doctrinal pitchfork. Each prong aims to skewer unwary Christians with false belief and faulty practice.

First, Paul warned against "the dogs." In that day, "dog" might describe any unclean animal, a prowler, a scavenger—or a Gentile. In short, it designated what was undesirable in Paul's society. Here the apostle used the term to refer to those who were clearly dangerous to the Christian community. How are we affected in this way today? We can understand Paul's anger, but we do not want to pick up on his name-calling. We must admit that there are still those in our society, both religious and secular, whose behavior and words can do us harm. Certainly Christians must watch out for such people today. Christians must beware of anyone who uses the good news of Jesus Christ and his liberating word to put others in bondage. Prime candidates for this watchfulness are those who use scripture to prescribe gender or racial roles for others, for example. Can you think of other modern-day "doglike" behaviors?

Paul warned about enemies of the cross in 3:18, and they were the second threat endangering the Philippians' spiritual well-being. Enemies likely were related to the "evil workers" of verse 2. These people may have been Judaizers who spread false teachings. Like their counterparts in Galatia and Colossae, they probably proclaimed that in order to be fully Christian, Gentile converts had to participate in Jewish rituals. Take a moment to read Galatians 4:8-20 and Colossians 2:8-19 to become more familiar with the kinds of religious beliefs and practice advocated by false teachers of the day.

A third source of spiritual endangerment probably came from evangelistic Jews—"those who mutilate the flesh" (3:2). These people could have been either lifelong Jews or new converts to Judaism who came to Philippi in order to convert Gentile Christians to Jewish Christianity. We can understand their insistence on following the ritual practices of the synagogue, especially that male converts must be circumcised. Apparently these teachers boasted that it was their circumcision, what Paul calls confidence in the flesh (3:3-4), that made them worthy of God's blessing. Such teaching, of course, contradicts the theology of salvation Paul preached. For Paul, salvation comes not through ritual but through faith in the Lord Jesus Christ.

A Better Way

In order to prove his point, Paul matched his credentials with those of the evangelistic Jews. First he pointed to the Christian believers as being the true circumcision, for they worshiped in the Spirit of God, boasted only in Christ Jesus, and had no confidence in the flesh (3:3-4). Then Paul said that there is no reason to have confidence in the flesh anyway. He used a play on words, referring to both circumcision and every other kind of human achievement. The irony is that Paul truly was a man of achievement by the standards he was abhorring.

Paul said, in effect, that he was a proud Jew down to the bottom of his soul—more Jewish than the folks who were disturbing the Philippians. As Paul described his background in 3:5-6, we realize that his credentials as a Jewish man were what he determined to forsake when he took on Christ. He actually counted his loss of that heritage as a great gain, for Christ had become of greatest value to him. We should not take this to mean, however, that Paul tossed away "junk" to gain Christ. And this text is ill used if we try to make it say that it means the end of Torah. No, Paul let go of something that was of great value to him in order to take hold of a better way. Christ surpassed everything of worth to him.

Paul gained a great prize: participation in the resurrection of Jesus. He wanted to keep growing in order to know the greatest possible faith in his Lord. Of course, what he wanted for himself he also wanted for everyone who believed his words. What, then, is the prize, or the call, for contemporary Christians?

A Worthy Goal

The prize for which we endure—toward which we run, pray, worship, and work—is that of being claimed by Christ in a tangible way. It is not a fuzzy universalism that says all of us are somehow automatically claimed by Christ. Rather, it is the conscious acceptance of an invitation to be Christ's own people and the intentional commitment to demonstrate that identity with good works in the world. In an increasingly complex and compact world, in which we are isolated by economics and technology, we long for security, for peace of mind, for connection. All of this is given to us in our heavenly citizenship (3:20) as we live it out in practical fellowship by helping one another, encouraging one another, praying for one another. I know this is true through personal experience. There was a time when I was in a vocational and personal crisis. What kept me going were the telephone calls, words of affirmation, and prayers that special friends offered to me and on my behalf.

The Philippians were proud citizens of a Roman colony and would understand Paul's language of citizenship in a distant place—like Rome—that they had never seen. Paul made the point that their sovereign was Jesus and that Jesus would do the work of transformation of their lives, beginning in the present and extending to eternity. That is the prize worth pursuing. Once gained, it is the prize worth holding tightly.

What keeps us pursuing the heavenly goal? It is the call from God for faithful living here and now: "Stand firm in the Lord" (4:1). For some people, that will mean standing with the poor and disenfranchised in their journey to liberation. For others, faithful living will mean caring for their families. For others it will be tithing, or being actively involved in neighborhood projects. The possibilities are endless, the reward is the same: to be called by God in Christ Jesus. Such a prize is worth all of the energy we can expend to attain it.

Discussion and Action

1. From your work in Personal Preparation, share some of your reasons for confidence. Name one or more of your spiritual gifts. Do other group members affirm your gifts?
2. Talk together about how you "know Christ" in your lives. What experiences of Christ's closeness can you share?
3. Paul seemed to be saying that although distractions to faithfulness will always be with us, our task is to stay focused even when it would be easier to give up or give in. What kinds of distractions threaten the church today? How do we keep going, even when we want to quit?
4. In what ways do you personally need endurance right now? What can you share about this with your group? Consider relating your response to the question about "giving up" in Personal Preparation.
5. How is life different, in practical terms, when we go through our daily routines with our "eyes on the prize"?
6. Paul spoke of those whose "god is the belly" (3:19). In this regard, C. S. Lewis wrote in *The Weight of Glory:* "If we consider the unblushing promises of reward and the staggering nature of the rewards promised in the gospels, it would seem that our Lord finds our desires, not too strong, but too weak. We are half-hearted creatures, fooling about with drink and sex and ambition when infinite joy is offered us, like an ignorant child who wants to go on making mud pies in a slum because he cannot imagine what is meant by the offer of a holiday at the sea. We are far too easily pleased." To what extent do you agree with Lewis? Can you offer a personal example of being too easily pleased? Why is it so tough to

avoid the temptation of easy pleasures? What helps you in the struggle to avoid temptation?

7. Do you think we are sometimes too quick to label aspects of our lives as opposing Christ? Or are we not quick enough to identify our opposition to Christ?
8. In 3:17, Paul offered himself as an example worthy of imitation. He did so in the tradition of teachers who serve as role models in the lives of their students. Who has been a role model for you in the past? Who are your role models now? Whom may you recommend, along with the Apostle Paul, as a hero of the faith for a young person in your church? Feel free to name some secular role models, too.

4

Inner Peace . . . Lived Out

Philippians 4:2-23

Paul closed his letter to the Philippians by lifting up the themes of reconciliation and peace. He wanted two church leaders to reconcile, to show what it means to experience the peace of God in every situation. All of this is possible—then and now—because of God's promise to meet the believer's every need.

Personal Preparation

1. Read Philippians 4:2-23. Take a moment to think of some experiential definitions of inner peace, for example, "Peace is being on a Florida beach in July," or, "Peace means not feeling guilty about taking a nap." In other words, how do you personally *experience* peace?
2. Recall a time when you felt most content. Was this a time when everything seemed to be going your way? Were you able to find inner contentment even when outward circumstances seemed threatening?
3. When have you found peace through prayer? Were your prayers answered? In what way?

Understanding

On the fiftieth anniversary of the Hiroshima and Nagasaki bombings, *The War Between Us* aired on television. This movie dealt with Japanese families who were forced to leave their homes on Canada's west coast after the Pearl Harbor attack. Two families, one of Japanese descent and the other of Irish descent, became neighbors. At first there was no apparent hope of these two families ever becoming friendly.

They knew so little about each other. The Irish family marveled that the Japanese could speak English, for example. The Japanese family, having come from urban Vancouver, was appalled at having to live in an underpopulated, interior town where many people had no electricity or gas stoves. Eventually reconciliation took place as the two families came to know and respect one another, but the pathway to reconciliation was watered with many tears and myriad disappointments.

How can peace blossom in the midst of pervasive and ongoing conflict? That was the question Paul faced as he closed out his correspondence to the Philippian church. We have no more understanding of the nature of the conflict than we had at the beginning of the letter. We do know that there was serious disagreement, because this portion of the letter begins with a plea for reconciliation.

Pursuing Reconciliation

Good news and bad news are both present. The good news is that women were leading in the church at Philippi, and Paul affirmed that leadership. In fact, Acts 16 reminds us that Lydia was the first Christian and leader of the Philippian house church. The bad news is that two women, Euodia and Syntyche, were engaged in a dispute serious enough for Paul to address, and it threatened the well-being of the church. If the leaders of a faith community cannot agree, how can they protect the integrity of their witness to the world?

Reconciliation remains the challenge and opportunity for the church of Jesus Christ today. It has been said, and confirmed in many of our congregations, that 11 A.M. on Sunday morning is the most segregated hour in the United States. Certainly we have our understandable doctrinal separations, but are we separated along racial, social, and economic lines, as well? Sometimes the answer is yes, for legitimate reasons. After all, there must be room in the church for different styles of worship and for different cultures to express their love for God in ways that seem best to them. However, when a stranger steps into our household of faith, especially a person who seems different from us, do we have a spirit of welcome rather than suspicion?

The roots of our inability to live as reconciled people run deep. They stem from misgivings based on race, gender, sexual orientation, income, and the need to be with "my own kind." A spirit of openness and tolerance that is both articulated and lived helps us overcome such barriers and become agents of reconciliation.

A sign in front of a church building reads, "Everyone is welcome." That is not at all unusual for a church sign, but I was struck by the next phrase: "Come as you are." Two meanings flow from such an open invitation. One is the recognition that not everyone can (or wants to) dress up for worship—this congregation is not overly concerned with clothing. The other is an invitation to enter the safety of this particular sanctuary *now* without having to "clean up" or "straighten out." We become agents of Christ's reconciliation when we determine to understand and embrace people who are enigmas to us. They do not have to change before we can begin a relationship. The congregation with a truly welcoming sign is living out the peace of God.

Finding Peace

What exactly is the peace of God? We may not be able to define it, but most of us could describe it. Perfect peace is likened to a hot bath after a trying day, a baseball game on a balmy summer night, or the warm embrace of a loved one. Peace can be a life lived with no overwhelming worries ("Do not worry about anything," 4:6). It is having friends, family, membership in a religious community, and the assurance of comfort in moments of grief and hardship. In a neighborhood, peace is a sense of safety. Peace may be as simple as being able to take a walk around the block after dark. For the church community, God's peace reigns when there is a foundation of trust and mutuality in fellowship.

What helps us achieve the peace of God? Perhaps it is most accurate to say that we simply learn to accept it. In 4:6-19 Paul gave several clues as to how he was able to settle down and live in the gift of God's peace.

First, *the peace of God begins in moments of prayer,* in conversations that speak to God of our deepest joys and fears. "In everything by prayer and supplication with thanksgiving let your requests be made known to God" (4:6). Prayer brings peace when we approach it in a way that truly asks, absolutely trusts, and completely yields our will through a process of discerning what it is that we need from God. It is more than wishful thinking. Prayer is a form of action. Someone has said that we should pray and then put legs on our prayers.

What might this active prayer look like? A congregation in a city near my home bought an apartment building and provides homes for men and women living with AIDS—people for whom the church members constantly pray. Another church opened its doors in a time of neighborhood tension and created space for poor and not-so-poor neighbors to talk with each other. Offering Bible study, stewardship education, outreach to special needs—or just making a friend in

Christ's name—are all ways of putting shoe leather on our prayers. There are endless possibilities for people and communities seeking the peace of God through active prayer and service.

Related to prayer is Paul's second clue to finding peace: *the peace of God flourishes with the right frame of mind* as we go through our daily routines. Paul encouraged the Philippians to think the most worthy thoughts, to continually focus on "whatever is true, whatever is honorable, whatever is just, whatever is pure, whatever is pleasing, whatever is commendable" (4:8). He offered himself as an example of this way of approaching life. "Keep on doing the things that you have learned and received and heard and seen in me, and the God of peace will be with you" (4:9). Paul did not invite his beloved Philippians to imitate him as if they were playing a kind of saintly Simon Says. He simply asked them to emulate his best qualities: his dependence on prayer, his willingness to stay focused on "anything worthy of praise" (4:8), and his unwavering confidence in God's provision. He wanted to see the same qualities blossoming in them that God had graciously cultivated in him.

As Paul brought his letter to a close, he offered a third clue to the inner peace he proclaimed: *the peace of God descends as we learn to accept things as they are.* Paul had reached a level of inner contentment that had nothing to do with external circumstances. "For I have learned to be content with whatever I have" (4:11). He declared his thankfulness for the Philippians' gift, but he would not have been defeated had they failed to come through for him. He had learned how to have peace without needing to control his life's agenda.

In the final analysis, true peace comes packaged with surrender to God. After all, how much control do we really have? I have found out that I cannot control when or whether my loved ones die, when I will lose a job, or when my next job will come. It is best, then, to approach each new day with this blessed realization: "My God will fully satisfy every need . . . according to his riches in glory in Christ Jesus" (4:19).

Discussion and Action

1. What are some of the real or potential conflicts among Christians in your community, church, or covenant group? What insights from Philippians 4 could you apply in practical ways to these problems?
2. What is your reaction to the discussion of prayer as *action?* When we seek God's will, is there a time to *act?* When do we

wait for God? What situation in your community or church calls for active prayer right now?

3. Of the eight things Paul encouraged the Philippians to think about in 4:8, which is most needed in your lives? Share together your answers to this question: What keeps your minds focused on spiritual realities in your daily routines?
4. Look again at Paul's amazing statements in 4:11-12. What, for you, is the secret of being content? When have you received what you longed for . . . and it was not enough? How can such disappointment help us cultivate the attitude of which Paul wrote?
5. How do you interpret the words, "I can do all things through him who strengthens me" (4:13)? If possible, share a personal example of something that seemed impossible, but was accomplished through God's strength.
6. Paul wanted to persuade the Philippians that peace would come from their remembering to rejoice always (4:4). To close this study of Philippians, sing the chorus, "Rejoice in the Lord Always." Try it in a round.

5

Treasure Here!

Colossians 1—2:5

Paul composed a hymn to help his readers understand Jesus as the fullest embodiment of God. In Christ the believers would find all the treasures of wisdom and knowledge, even though certain false teachers were proclaiming a deeper wisdom. Even today we must watch out for those who dilute the message of Christ's supremacy in all things.

Personal Preparation

1. Read through Colossians 1—2:5 and then focus your thoughts on the "Christ Hymn" of verses 15-20. What can you discover about the nature and work of Christ from this passage of scripture alone? Jot a list of some of those things.
2. Spend some quiet time prayerfully completing this sentence: "Jesus, to me you are . . . . " Rather than writing a response, you may wish to draw a picture or sing a hymn that expresses your feelings.
3. What does the "Lordship" of Jesus mean to you personally? Think: If someone were to make a movie documentary of your life so far, what scenes would show your most cherished priorities or loyalties? How would these scenes relate to lordship?

Understanding

In Robert Louis Stevenson's *Treasure Island,* young Jim Hawkins steals away aboard the pirate ship *Hispaniola* with a few mutinous men. Intent on finding buried treasure, they have a map from Captain Billy Bones displaying a large red X. The words next to that mysterious marker would send shivers of anticipation down any pirate's spine: "Bulk of Treasure Here."

We Christians also have our "big red X": Christ himself, Christ the one "in whom are hidden all the treasures of wisdom and knowledge" (2:3). The treasure does not stay hidden, for the book of Colossians—a gleaming gem in the New Testament—clearly divulges "the riches of the glory of this mystery, which is Christ in you, the hope of glory" (1:27). In its Christ-hymn (1:15-20) we uncover the great treasure of Colossians: the Bible's most ringing affirmation of the sovereignty of Jesus Christ. Along with this book's sacred treasure, however, we also discover evidence of spiritual treachery. Certain false teachers were tempting the Colossian church with a different gospel.

Irreconcilable Differences

The Colossian congregation was not begun by Paul, although he did visit the area on one of his missionary journeys. From that visit the good news of Jesus Christ spread. At the time Paul wrote his letter to the Christians of Colossae, probably around 60 A.D., the city was like most metropolitan areas of North America in terms of its cultural and religious diversity. Today we may find a large, new evangelical church on one corner, across the street an Islamic temple, nearby a gleaming Buddhist shrine, and several storefront churches downtown. Paul's letter was concerned with what can result from such situations: the blurring of lines between religions.

The Colossians needed to know that the Christian faith was irreconcilable with some of the teachings offered to them. Paul clearly did not want his brothers and sisters to be victims of deceptive teachers—doctrinal pirates, in effect, who might take them captive (2:8) with plausible heresies. His dilemma was the same as that faced by church leaders today as they try to maintain faithfulness and integrity in the midst of religious pluralism.

The precise nature of the false teaching is unclear, but Paul's defense of the faith was fierce. We can be sure he was defending his belief in the centrality of Jesus Christ in the church. Apparently some church members were incorporating different religious practices into the practice of Christianity. They observed special days on their calendars related to astronomical signs or prescribed certain diets in conjunction with god-myths and festival periods. Such syncretism (the co-mingling of religious beliefs) would push Jesus out of the center of the church. He would become just one of many spiritual personalities to be honored.

Syncretism is not the same as ecumenism, which seeks to bring together different Christian communions. Nor is syncretism the same as interreligious dialog or other activities in which the integrity of each religious perspective is maintained and respected while groups work together with a common interest. Paul was concerned with a kind of creeping inter-mixing of beliefs that would harm the body of Christ. The Colossian practices minimized the preeminent role of Christ, the one who must have "first place in everything" (1:18).

Reconciling Reminders

Some beliefs are clearly irreconcilable with Christian belief, as Paul declared. In other respects, however, Paul spoke in favor of reconciliation. How were the Colossians, and all believers, reconciled? Paul listed some of the ways in 1:9-23, for example:

> [He] has enabled you to share in the inheritance of the saints in the light. He has rescued us from the power of darkness and transferred us into the kingdom of his beloved Son. . . . And through him God was pleased to reconcile to himself all things . . . by making peace through the blood of his cross. And you who were once estranged and hostile in mind, he has now reconciled in his fleshly body through death, so as to present you holy and blameless and irreproachable before him. (1:12-13, 20-21)

Paul called this congregation away from vague, false teachings by speaking of reconciliation, by reminding them of "who and whose" they were. *We, too, can benefit from such reminders.* First, 1:9-14 reminded the Colossians that they were not alone, that others were praying for them. South African Bishop Desmond Tutu often said that in the long years leading to Nelson Mandela's election, the prayers of Christians all over the world held steady the freedom-loving people of South Africa. In our passage Paul and his companions offered steadying prayers of strength for the Colossians that through Jesus Christ they would come to know the will of God. Such knowledge would yield marvelous benefits: fulfilled ministries, increased knowledge of God, endurance for their souls, and a spirit of joyful thanksgiving.

In 1:15-20 Paul offered the church a hymn about the person of Christ, a definitive counterpoint to the deadly idea that Jesus was merely one among any number of heavenly intermediaries. The hymn reminded the Colossians that their almighty God was reflected in the presence of Jesus. God is at the center of the world and it is Jesus as the picture of God who helps us understand the world. As followers of Christ, we too are called to bear the likeness of God in our words and actions.

The Son of God shines forth in majestic terms. He is the image of the invisible God, the firstborn of creation, the vehicle of all that exists. He is before all things, the head of the church, first among the resurrected, the one in whom "all the fullness of God was pleased to dwell" (1:19). This sublime Jesus is the principal agent of reconciliation, through his blood, for the sake of heaven and earth. What a treasure he is! If Paul were in a debate, we might say that he laid out his case for Christ in magnificent fashion, showing exactly why this Savior occupies the seat at the right hand of God (3:1). The apostle left little room for further discussion. In Colossians, Christ is raised up and remains so for all eternity.

In 1:21-23 Paul told church members what the hymn meant for them. He reminded them that they were converted, saved from their sin, and redeemed by Christ Jesus. Their call was to continue to be faithful to the genuine gospel they first heard, instead of the counterfeit gospel they were currently hearing.

Recognized Commission

If Christ is the *means* of reconciliation and believers are the *object* of reconciliation, then we might view Paul as the *subject* of reconciliation in 1:24—2:5. That is, Paul carried the message as a servant of the mystery. For Paul, the great truths about Christ issued in one thing: to become the church's "servant according to God's commission. . . . For this I toil and struggle with all the energy that he powerfully inspires within me" (1:25, 29).

In what ways are we, too, commissioned by the message of the fullness of God in Christ? One way is through struggling, just as Paul struggled, on behalf of others. This surely involves evangelism ("It is he whom we proclaim," 1:28), but it also involves a striving for fairness and justice in the world. One of the ways we live out our faith is by doing justice to others and by holding ourselves and others accountable when justice is not done. Our commission also involves the challenge we face when attempting to build loving relationships with our neighbors, family members, and communities of faith.

In this regard, Paul once again offered himself as an example for the church just as he did in Philippians 4. He modeled a way of living as a servant of the gospel. He suffered and struggled for the sake of the church, having landed in prison for witnessing to his faith. Like him, we are the bearers of Christ in our own world. Christ is our "hope of glory" (1:27).

Discussion and Action

1. Share your movie scenes from Personal Preparation question 3. Why is it difficult to describe clearly what the Lordship of Christ means in every believer's life?
2. Focus on 1:1-14. How would you describe the relational context for Paul's theological statements to the Colossians?
3. Meditate for a moment on Colossians 1:16, then react to this quotation from Albert Camus, the existentialist philosopher: "Up till now man [sic] derived his coherence from his Creator. But from the moment that he consecrated his rupture with him, he finds himself delivered over to the passing days, and to wasted sensibility." What evidence do you see in your community that people have "consecrated" a sense of separation from God? How can the church help heal that rupture in practical ways?
4. What insights regarding environmental issues may be discovered in Colossians 1, especially verse 20? What does reconciliation mean with regard to the environment?
5. Work together to develop short lists of groups that consider themselves Christian but that you would not identify as Christian. What groups would you list as Christian? What, in your opinion, marks these groups as Christian or non-Christian? Relate your response to the statements about Christ in 1:15-23.
6. As a group project, write a Christ-hymn for today. Include in it a "grandest" statement about Christ and a "simplest" statement about Christ.
7. Colossians 1:15-20 is one of several christological passages in the New Testament. If your group has time, consider looking at other passages and discussing how they add to the picture of Christ. Suggested passages are John 1:1-18; Philippians 2:5-11; Hebrews 1:1-4; Hebrews 2:10-18; Ephesians 1:3-23; and Revelation 5:9-14.

6

Warning: Hazardous to Your (Spiritual) Health!

Colossians 2:6-23

Paul challenged his readers to continue in Christ, "established in the faith" (2:7). The Colossian Christians had to be alert to false philosophies that detracted from the fullness of Christ. Then and now, countless varieties of legalism and speculation can be hazardous to Christian growth.

Personal Preparation

1. Read Colossians 2:6-23. Has a friend or acquaintance ever presented a clearly erroneous idea to you as though it were a religious truth? How did you respond? How *would* you respond, should this occur in the future?
2. What guidelines could you offer someone in a similar circumstance? That is, how can we disagree with ideas without rejecting relationships?
3. In a moment of quiet reflection, consider the boundaries of Christian belief. How do I know what is essential and what is not, in matters of faith?

Understanding

At an open house for a member of my church, I met another guest who said that she was born into one denomination, became part of another when she got married, and now was not a regular churchgoer at all. She was, however, intrigued by the philosophy of a certain "spiritual teacher" whom she named and praised. "After all," she said, "we will all wind up in the same place, so it really doesn't matter whether we talk about Jesus, Buddha, or Krishna—or whether God is simply to be found in these flowers. It's all the same."

Confronting Error

How can we hold to common theological understandings while honoring diverse movements in the church? How can we live in Christian unity in an increasingly diverse culture?

As Paul wrote to the Colossians, he too faced such questions but he wanted his readers to remember what they had been taught and to continue living in faithfulness to Christ Jesus (2:6). This relationship with Christ was no casual, tenuous connection. Paul used concrete words to describe it: "rooted," "built up," and "established." As used here in 2:7, "established" has contractual implications. It means that believers enjoyed a relationship ratified by their baptism and bound by their pledge of faithfulness to God.

Paul then used an image in 2:8 that came from a rather humiliating practice of the Romans. Conquering generals took their captives and forced them through the city streets chained to the victors' chariots and dragged along behind. Paul wanted the Colossians to beware of being taken captive by men and women who would add to or detract from the "fullness" of Jesus Christ—and from the fullness of living their lives in him. Such teachings, what we are calling "the Colossian heresy," consisted of four key errors.

First, Paul wrote of the error of *false philosophy* in 2:8-15. Does this mean that Christians should not study the great philosophers, past and present? Of course not, for even our theology can have a philosophical underpinning, ascribe to certain presuppositions, and hold to a particular worldview that determines its starting point. What Paul wanted his readers to avoid was any teaching that called into question the reality of revealed truth: Jesus incarnate as the "whole fullness of deity" (2:9).

Second, Paul warned of the error of *legalism* (2:16-17). Both Jewish religious leaders and gentile cultists had their calendars of special days filled with sacred rituals. To celebrate or not to celebrate was not the heart of the issue for Paul. The point was that such things neither produced nor extended the kingdom of God in any sense. Only Jesus extends the Kingdom, for he is its "substance."

Third, the practice of *angel worship* must not lead believers astray (2:18-19). If there was an element of Gnosticism in the Colossian heresy, then this reference to angels is understandable. Gnostics explained how God could create a world that had evil and suffering in it. They envisioned a hierarchy of angelic beings existing between the "evil" world and the "spiritual" heavens. God created everything through these beings, keeping God untouched by evil. Gnostics supposedly humbled themselves by worshiping these beings instead of the Creator. In other words, the Gnostics viewed themselves as too lowly to approach God directly. Of course, Paul said that this indirect and falsely humble approach to God only caused such worshipers to be "puffed up without cause by a human way of thinking" (2:18).

The fourth error was *asceticism* (2:20-23). Again, a Gnostic philosophy would say that because the body is evil, it must be denied all pleasure: "Do not handle, Do not taste, Do not touch" (2:21). The Gnostics thought that by inflicting deprivation on the body, the life of the spirit could grow. Again Paul said no! Although ascetic practices may appear to be wise, "they are of no value in checking self-indulgence" (2:23).

In light of these ancient errors, we might ask what Paul would have to say to the contemporary church. We, too, are faced with myriad philosophies and movements that can subvert the gospel. Examples include cults with defective christologies, New Age philosophies that combine Eastern mysticism with legitimate Christian contemplative practices, movements with selected Christian values and litmus tests of orthodoxy, highly individualistic spiritualities that ignore the community, civil religion that identifies the church with any one culture, and human-centered fulfillment as the highest religious goal. To be alert to such things requires the fine art of Christian discernment.

Learning Discernment

The conversation that opened this chapter caused the pastor to ask herself a critical question: *What are the boundaries of Christian belief?* She recalled what she had been taught and realized that she typically filters ideas through a fourfold grid, evaluating them in terms of scripture, experience, tradition, and reason.

Such an approach to discernment is vital for the church as Christians try to distinguish between true and false teaching. In our day—as in Paul's—false teachers and their exciting lessons flourish because we live among spiritually empty and hungry people. Many are vulnerable to promises that offer to fill that gaping, inner void. With wise discernment we must constantly ask, What is a false teacher?

False teachers likely speak little of the common good. They often preach and teach self-serving philosophies while receiving benefits they do not deserve. They are the ones who gain power when others fight. In the church, they are prone to teach cheap grace and easy salvation based on rules and tests that can be evaluated by all observers. On the one hand, they may be extreme literalists who use the Bible to support their legalisms as a list of "dos and don'ts"; on the other hand, they may give no primacy to the Bible and support an uncomplicated salvation for all. False teachers are less servants of the church than captives of a personal agenda that uses the church as a means to an end.

Legitimate disagreements *will* arise in the church, however, conflicts that have only subtle connections to the question of truth and error. Recall, for example, the 1995 celebrations related to the anniversary of World War II. Memories surfaced, as did emotions that were filled with pride and dread. A conscientious objector who went to prison during that war remembers 1945 differently than a soldier who stormed the ramparts of Berlin. And the soldier's memories differ from those of a nurse who suffered through a Pacific island prison camp. These experiences, clearly different, should be respected. We must sort out those situations of conflict that include, on both sides, members of a single congregation.

In raising the question of truth and error, we raise many other practical and hard-to-answer questions as well. How do we live in community while seeking to deepen the faith of people who label themselves liberal or conservative—terms that often are divisive in the church? Is there a common message for an advocate of arms-bearing and the church member who advocates gun control? How do pro-life and pro-choice people talk to one another during coffee hour? What is the best way to discuss the role of women in the church, or the different ways of understanding family values? We need to discern how best to live with such questions because diversity makes up the rich fabric of the church. Our differing gifts are a given in the kingdom.

Disagreeing Without Rejecting

One of the earliest lessons taught to me in Sunday school was that God loves everyone and wants what is best for them. Sometimes I find myself humming the old gospel song "Jesus loves the little children," no matter what the color of their skin. I think about the members of my congregation who became Christians as adults, how they have testified to the church as a place where they feel accepted, where they can ask questions and receive answers without feeling judged.

I know that it is not enough just to ferret out theological error and to try to avoid the human hurt that loving confrontation can cause. Somehow I must seek reconciliation and maintain fellowship, because diversity is a gift from heaven. We are each made in God's image, a thronging variety of people, united with Christ in baptism, who are growing "with a growth that is from God" (2:19). I must learn to disagree with specious ideas while refusing to reject Christ's precious people.

Discussion and Action

1. What would you have said to the woman in the opening story of this session? How would you respond if a friend or acquaintance presented a clearly erroneous idea to you as though it were a tenet of Christian theology?
2. How can we disagree with ideas without rejecting relationships? What guidelines would you suggest?
3. In 2:8 we find an unusual phrase describing the Colossian heresy: "according to the elemental spirits of the universe." Some have suggested that this refers to the practice of astrology. Do you have any neighbors or co-workers who look to astrology to guide them? What do you say when someone asks, "What sign are you?"
4. In 2:11, what Christ did for us is termed "spiritual circumcision." This may refer to Christ's death and our "death" with him in baptism. Talk about your own baptism. When did it take place? Where? What did it mean then? What does it mean to you today?
5. Describe some of the attractions and pitfalls, from observation or experience, of an ascetic lifestyle, an interest in angels, charismatic leaders, and New Age ideas. In what ways could you describe such things as a shadow next to the substance of the gospel message (2:17)?
6. What are some of your own litmus tests of true belief? What are some of your congregation's tests? What are some of your denomination's tests of faith? To what extent are these tests valid in light of today's scripture?
7. Spencer Perkins, an African American church leader, said in *More Than Equals:* "Christianity doesn't require any power when its only challenge is to do something that already comes naturally. But it will take a powerful gospel—a gospel with guts—to enable us to love across all the barriers we erect to edify our own kind and protect us from our insecurities." What is your reaction to this statement? In what way is our tendency to erect barriers in the church—whether stemming from race or theology—based on our insecurity? What remedies to this predicament can you suggest?

7

Put On Those Heavenly Clothes

Colossians 3:1-17

Paul offered the Colossians practical advice on how to live a Christian lifestyle. He used the image of changing clothes to highlight the transformation that occurs when the old self has been stripped off and we put on Christ.

Personal Preparation

1. Silently read Colossians 3:1-17. When have you seen love keeping church members together despite different lifestyle decisions?
2. Focus on 3:13. Have you ever extended forgiveness to someone out of pure grace? How did it make you feel? How did the forgiven person respond?
3. Envision your spiritual life as a wardrobe full of clothes. How would you describe the items of clothing? Jot down some adjectives (in fashion-designer lingo) that you could bring to your covenant group meeting. Feel free to use humor, for example: "I have a pair of comfy 'flip-flops' because sometimes I change my mind about taking time for prayer," or "My sleek, genuine leather vest reminds me of God's protection when I'm tempted."

Understanding

Last Easter Sunday, ten-year-old Shawn was baptized along with several other people who completed the church's membership class. After the service, as he was drying off, he gazed into the mirror. He was trying to see whether he looked any different than before he stepped into the lukewarm water in front of his family and friends. *Will people know, just by looking at me, that I'm different now?* Shawn knew that he enjoyed a brand-new relationship with God and the church—and he wanted to know if it showed.

According to the Apostle Paul, yes, it definitely *should* show! Certain kinds of behavior ought to mark the Christian as different. In the last session we asked, What are the boundaries of Christian belief? This week we rephrase the question: What are the boundaries of Christian *lifestyle?*

Taking Off

Paul answered the question by reminding the Colossians of their new, exalted position with Christ. Just as they rose up out of the baptismal waters, they have been raised up in union with Christ. Now that they were transformed on the inside through the forgiveness of sins (1:14), they ought to have been displaying certain outward changes. What follows, then, are lists of behaviors to be discarded by the Colossians because already they "stripped off the old self" (3:9).

The first list, in 3:5-7, has to do with sexual and moral issues. Paul used strong language in urging believers to lay aside what some would call sins of the flesh although actually they are "sins of humanness": "fornication, impurity, passion, evil desire, and greed." Such behavior laces the plots of too many of our movies, television dramas, and radio talk shows. Many groups and individuals understand such behavior to be a prime sign of the moral decay in our society. They point to unmarried couples living together, young teenagers having babies, countless people greedily grasping at all they can get because, as one bumper sticker proclaims, "The one who dies with the most toys . . . WINS!"

Paul made the point that if we are engaged with the risen Christ, we also are engaged with each other. He called the church away from anything that would violate the relationships formed with God and with our brother and sister Christians. Sexual sins are a violation of our most intimate and sacred commitments. The deepest pain in such behavior is caused by a foundational infidelity to our promises. Greed or covetousness, which can be understood as the desire always to have a bit more, can lead us to value objects more than we value people. Human devaluing becomes obvious as we see the growing numbers of homeless and displaced people walking our streets.

Greed is more subtle, but no less destructive, when people use their resources to maintain fragile, superficial lifestyles. For instance, a national news story featured families living in huge houses—with no furniture. They were not waiting for the sofa to be delivered; they simply could not pay the huge mortgage, send their children to private school, maintain memberships at the country club, buy the right clothes . . . and have chairs and beds, too!

The next set of verses, 3:8-9, have to do with the moral power of our words. By encouraging the Colossians to discard speech that is angry, wrathful, malicious, slanderous, and abusive, Paul debunked the old maxim many of us chanted as children: "Sticks and stones may break my bones, but words can never hurt me." The bright-eyed little girl whose parents tell her she is stupid, the man who overhears his pastor revealing a shared secret, the businesswoman who is told she is "too aggressive for a lady" all know the power of words to wound as deeply as a sharp blade slicing to the bone.

Words matter. Think of the lift to your spirits when someone offers a sincere compliment. All of our actions are subject to critique and none of us can expect to be commended all of the time, but when someone belittles our best efforts with words that cannot help us improve, which serve only to humiliate and devalue us, that person has practiced a significant evil. Paul wanted his readers to know that there is simply no place in the church for harmful self-indulgence or destructive speech.

Putting On

What did Paul want the church to do? Using the analogy of putting on new clothes, he called believers to live out the new life by adopting life-enhancing behaviors. In effect, he said, you have taken off your old, detrimental clothes. Here are some new ones for you to put on; they will make you feel like the new person in Christ Jesus that you actually are.

The new self is in the process of being renewed as it grows in knowledge of God. As renewal occurs, interpersonal barriers that have divided people and communities break down. For Paul, Christ was the presence and the power responsible for wiping out any impediment to community, since "Christ is all and in all" (3:11).

Having removed spiritually damaging and ragged clothes, the church members could now clothe themselves in fine, virtuous linens. Thus Paul offered another behavior-clothing list. In 3:12-14, after reminding the people that they were God's chosen ones, Paul lifted up behavior that is compassionate, kind, humble, meek, and patient. These things are not always easy to achieve, and pursuing them brings us to the precipice of temptation. Indeed, we can easily slip into the lure of their opposites, returning to the kind of lifestyle condemned in 3:5-9. It surely is true that enmity, meanness, vanity, a will that is too strong, and impatience can all lead to selfish indulgence. When that happens, and failure leads to relational pain, we must seek to give our best selves to one another again—forgiving as we have been forgiven.

Words about forgiveness are appropriate, for Paul knew that even among Christians there would be conflict. After all, that is one of the prime reasons Paul wrote to the Colossian Christians. They were called to learn to bear with each other, but on those occasions when harm was done, to extend the grace that forgives.

Verse 14 offers the final and most important garment to be included in the Colossians' spiritual wardrobe: love. As they put on love, they had an excellent chance to be bound together in the kind of harmony only God can provide. A result of love in the community is heartfelt peace and a sense of gratitude to God, who has brought the people together through Jesus Christ. If the peace of Christ rules in our hearts, we look to what is best for the whole community rather than settling for what is good only for a few individuals.

Paul closed this list of practical advice by calling on believers to listen to and absorb the word of Christ. The apostle was a strong advocate of the community—"to which indeed you were called in the one body" (3:15)—as a place of worship. During this time of honoring God, teaching takes place. Presumably Paul's advice will be affirmed as members support and critique each other. Joyful songs ring out, and the people share in communion. The gratitude with which believers come to worship reaches its peak through every word, song, and prayer offered in the name of Jesus Christ.

Paul used some provocative words and phrases: "raised up with Christ" (3:1), "put to death" (3:5), "get rid of" (3:8), "stripped off the old self" (3:9), "clothed yourselves" (3:10), "renewal" (3:11), "God's chosen ones" (3:12). What does all of this mean? Among other things, such language says that the standard for Christian living is high. Paul expected church members to aim at meeting that standard. Just as important as the pursuit of that high calling is the recognition that individuals are not striving alone. Thankfully, we can trust that our fellow members in Christ's body will catch us when we fall short of the goal . . . and bid us try once again to meet it.

Discussion and Action

1. What words or phrases in the Bible text stand out as the key to living a holy life? Share the things that support you in your attempts to live out this Christian lifestyle, day by day. What helps you the most? What are some of the greatest hindrances?
2. Together name some examples of lifestyle disagreements that have led to the things listed in 3:8. What role does love play in discerning the boundaries of Christian lifestyle and resolving such conflicts (3:14)? Can you share a story about the working of love in this regard, when love seemed to keep church members together even when they disagreed about lifestyle issues?
3. What does it mean to do something "in the name of the LORD Jesus" (3:17)? Share practical examples from home and church life.
4. Recall the activity suggested in Personal Preparation question 3. How did you describe your "spiritual wardrobe" in fashion-designer terms? What old clothing have you put off over the years? What new clothes have you put on?
5. Talk together about the "good clothes"—Christian virtues listed in the text—you have seen each other displaying lately. Make this a time of affirmation and thankfulness.
6. Think about Paul's words related to forgiveness. If you know anyone in your group or congregation who feels alienated or hurt, hold that person in your thoughts during a brief period of silence. Then discuss, without naming any names, practical forms of love and forgiveness you as individuals or as a group can extend to those who hurt. Determine to take action this week, as a group or as individuals.

8

Family Life Yesterday and Today

Colossians 3:18—4:1

Having urged the Colossians to do everything in the name of Christ Jesus (3:17), Paul reminded the church of how its faith in Jesus affected its home and family life.

Personal Preparation

1. Read Colossians 3:18—4:1. Think about the family or home in which you grew up. How would you describe it? How does its influence still affect you today—for better or worse?
2. What is your definition of a family? How would you say the family has changed in the last ten years? How has your own definition of family changed?
3. Consider the Apostle Paul's apparent acceptance of slavery. How do you, personally, deal with his words?

Understanding

If a pollster came to your door and asked you to describe a typical family, what would you say? Would you describe a two-parent family? If so, would the two parents both be the biological or adoptive parents of all children in the house? Could the family consist of a single mother with one or more children? Might grandparents and other relatives be in the household? Would there be a single breadwinner and a work-at-home parent?

What is a family in these last days of the twentieth century? Colossians 3:18—4:1, along with other New Testament parallels (for example, Eph. 5:22—6:9; 1 Tim. 2:8-15 and 6:1-2; and 1 Peter 2:13—3:7) call up strong emotions in many people of faith. Some feel anger at the apparent subordination of women and children and at the apparently accepting attitude toward slavery. Other people feel a sense of satisfaction that their beliefs about the "correct" structure of the family are biblically affirmed. Both kinds of readers fail to grasp a crucial interpretive principle: we need not conform our twentieth-century *Christian experience* to a first-century *societal world view.*

Yesterday's Family

What was that first-century household like? How was it different from today's? Typically, it consisted of parents and their unmarried children. The household contained other relatives—such as uncles, aunts, grandparents—along with slaves and long-term visitors. The family was the primary place of socialization in the community and larger society. There, children learned the customs and stories of the family including (for the Jews) the story of God's dealings with the people of Israel. Legal authority in the family belonged almost exclusively to the father. He maintained control over the children until they married and began their own households.

The Greco-Roman structure of the family and its household codes seem to be reflected in our text. The New Testament holds Jesus' teachings in tension with Paul's in this area. For instance, Jesus both approved of the commandment to honor one's father and mother and said that loyalty to the family is subordinate to loyalty to the gospel (see, for instance, Matt. 10:35-37). The Christian community is a new kind of family.

How does the Bible deal with slavery? Some passages describe how the owner is to be compensated when a slave is injured by a third party. Such passages clearly view slaves as a form of property. Several other passages look at the master-slave relationship in a way that focuses on the humanity of the slave. It may help us to remember that both the treatment of slaves and the treatment of wives and children belonged to a set of accepted domestic codes. Paul added a crucial component: mutual submission to Christ's Lordship (3:23-24). These household codes served a purpose for the church in that they allowed Paul to address people in terms and structures they understood.

Today's Challenge

What do we make of these codes in the church and in society today? Surely we believe that strong, healthy families are a good thing. On the other hand, are "traditional" families, or even extended families, the only models of healthy, strong families? We may have passed the time when we can talk honestly about an exclusive model of family, because both healthy and dysfunctional families exist in myriad configurations in our neighborhoods and churches. We need never feel superior or defensive about how our families are formed. Nevertheless, many of us may resist the strictly defined roles suggested in these verses of Colossians.

These codes remind us of our ambivalence about social structures. We want to feel secure, but we rightly abhor the idea of living in a police state. In the same way, we want strong families but strict household codes remind us too much of repressive admonitions to people to stay in their place. We are left feeling uneasy.

For the church, the challenge is correct and life-giving interpretation. Except for some white supremacist organizations, no church urges a return to slavery as practiced in the United States in the last century. Nor does the church advocate a return to slavery as practiced in the first century. Many churches thriving in membership and meaningful programs, however, teach and preach support for a strictly patriarchal view of the family How can this be? We have come to know that slavery is inherently abusive and dehumanizing. Should we not also recognize that an authoritarian, iron-fisted patriarchy is as damaging to the souls of women, children, and men as is slavery? Both wrongly claim from God a right of domination that does not exist. We are all created in the image and likeness of God.

When the Colossians passage is interpreted narrowly, it is used to justify the kind of abuse we now call domestic violence. The passage seems to offer cover for men who abuse their wives, excuse the harming of children, and help rationalize the ugliest forms of racism. Whenever anyone claims absolute authority over another human being, especially in a family situation, evil lurks. The potential for shattered trust increases in proportion to the lack of mutual respect among all members of the household. No doubt the Apostle Paul's own guiding principle in family matters comes through most clearly in his great summarizing principle offered to the Ephesians: "Be subject to one another out of reverence for Christ" (5:21).

Tomorrow's Reward

Reverence for Christ, our "Master in heaven" (4:1), is the key. What does it mean for a family to work "for the LORD" (3:23), knowing that its members will "receive the inheritance as your reward" (3:24)? These are key verses, for they tie everything we are and do to "the LORD Christ" we serve (3:24).

Family life under the Lordship of Christ may mean for you what it means for me. I was raised in a Christian household where I learned early that God loves each of us and that God and our parents expect the best from us. This meant being taught the difference between right and wrong—and therefore acting as if I knew the difference. It meant that my parents took me to church and Sunday school. Growing up in a Christian household meant prayers before meals and before bed. It meant caring for the other members of the family and for our neighbors, even when they were not nice to us. It meant that my parents saw to it that we children were educated—academically, socially, and spiritually.

My parents' love and respect for each other was evident all of their married life. Discipline occasionally involved one or both of them saying to us children, "I'm the Mom/Dad, that's why!" Neither parent said to the other, "God has put me in charge, always." My parents' approach provided a model for relationships in which both partners work together for the purpose of helping the whole family grow strong. It was a household of clearly defined roles, but very little sense of superiority or inferiority. All of the children grew up with a sense of identity and strength. Ours was by no means a problem-free family, but it was a safe place. It has enabled me to stand firmly on early foundations of mutual love and respect.

Discussion and Action

1. How do you and your family members make decisions and determine direction in your family? Share any methods or principles that have helped you.
2. Ask any parents in your group how they apply 3:21. What does it mean, in day-to-day living, to discipline children while not embittering them?
3. Talk with your group about the parts of the Bible you or the church ignore, if any. Could 3:22 and 4:1 qualify? How should we interpret the master-slave language? Should it be relegated to a cultural situation that no longer applies? What indirect applications could be made from such passages?
4. In small groups or with partners, do a study of the parallel passages in the New Testament that are listed at the beginning of the Understanding section. What added insights about Christian family life come from these passages?
5. As a whole group, respond to this statement by Nelson Mandela, made at his trial on April 20, 1964: "I have fought against white domination, and I have fought against black domination. I have cherished the ideal of a democratic and

free society in which all persons will live together in harmony and with equal opportunities. It is an ideal which I hope to live for and achieve. But, if needs be, it is an ideal for which I am prepared to die." For what causes would you, yourself, be willing to die?

6. Define a "strong" versus "weak" family life. What are the families like in your group, church, and neighborhood? What is needed to make and keep all of them strong?

9

Keep on Witnessing
Colossians 4:2-18

Paul closed his letter to the Colossians with words of advice about their life of devotion, encouraging them to keep on praying and witnessing. Their behavior to other people—both inside and outside the church—would have great effect on the spread of the message about "the mystery of Christ" (4:3).

Personal Preparation

1. Read Colossians 4:2-18. What kind of witness brought you into the kingdom of God? Who was most influential in your conversion and growth in Christ?
2. How would you describe your prayer life? Spend a few moments in prayer each day as you prepare for your covenant group meeting.
3. In what ways do you witness to your faith? What kinds of circumstances might prevent you from being a witness?

Understanding

A little boy became afraid during a late-night hailstorm that beat down on his house. After a deafening roar of thunder, he leapt out of bed and burst into his parents' bedroom. Jumping into the bed between Mom and Dad, he sought protection and assurance. "Don't worry, Son," his father said. "Don't you know the Lord will keep you safe?"

The little boy scrunched up closer to his father and said, "I know, Dad, but right now I need somebody with skin on!"

It is crucial for all of us to know that we are loved, to be able to know why, and to *feel* it. The Apostle Paul loved his people. While he was away, he wanted them to know and feel that he loved them. Evidence of that love shines through his willingness to share his high expectations for their conduct. He spoke of their family duties (3:18—4:1). Now he would close with final exhortations regarding how they ought to continue in their spiritual growth through the religious duties of witnessing and prayer.

The Power of Witness

Witnesses speak from personal experience about what has happened to them or to others they have observed. In the New Testament the term *witness* refers primarily to those who attest to the truth about God. Interestingly, the word *martyr* is derived from the same Greek root word as witness. From his prison cell, Paul was a true witness, attesting to God's transforming power in his own life largely through his response to personal hardship. Perhaps he indeed became a literal martyr for his faith. No one knows for sure whether he was eventually acquitted or sentenced to death. Paul's example demonstrates the power that flows from a believer's willingness to witness to the faith in all circumstances. Such a witness makes following Jesus compelling and desirable, not because it is an easy way of life but because it is a life filled with purpose and meaning.

Whether we call it witnessing or evangelism, we ought not forget its simple essence: it is the act of one hungry person telling another hungry person where to find bread. This is how we are called to witness in the world, through meeting needs with loving words and actions. As William Barclay said, "Few people have ever been argued into Christianity."

In some parts of the world, to be a witness in the church of Jesus Christ is to choose martyrdom. That is seldom the case in the United States or other western nations, yet even here the call to witness means being a person whose faith colors and shapes every activity of daily life.

What, specifically, is the character of our witness? First, we witness with positive passion. We tell the church's story out of deeply held beliefs. Beliefs not only demonstrate our understanding of our faith but also shape our identity as a people with a purpose. Whether we hand out tracts on the street corner or worship on a weekly basis and do very little else, our call is to witness *for* something and not merely against certain things. For some of us perhaps too much of our political life and more than a little of our church decision-making are based on what we do *not* believe—or the people we are against—rather than on what we do believe and the people we can support.

Second, we witness with joy and hope. Philippians is a joyful letter and Colossians, at its heart, glows with the hope that Christ's church will be courageous enough to grow in its faithfulness. Ultimately our witness to the world is grounded in our unwavering faith in Jesus Christ, the One who is alive and at work in our midst. He is the source of our joy and hope. Paul's proclamation that our lives are intimately connected reflects such grounding. Paul's reference to "the mystery of Christ" (4:3) is a vivid reminder that we are all one in the body of Christ, every barrier broken down by his cross (see Eph. 2:16 and 3:5-6).

Practical Advice

Paul wrote to encourage believers to empower and support each other in their witness. They are brothers and sisters in Christ, and they can benefit from practical advice about how to live together in the world.

First, believers must remain devoted to praying for each other with thanksgiving. They were urged to pray not just for themselves, but for the sake of the proclamation of the Gospel, "to open . . . a door for the word" (4:3). Even from his prison cell Paul found an occasion for proclaiming the good news.

Next, the apostle urged the church members to practice good manners. Paul invited them to speak kindly to outsiders so that non-Christians would know, through the blessing of gracious speech and loving conduct, that they were among God's people. This is how the church extends its welcome: "Come, participate with us as members in the faith community." It is a call not to join a righteous elite but simply to gather with fellow sinners who are responding to divine acceptance.

In all of Paul's instructions, we recognize the practical goal of witnessing: to make the gospel attractive to people who hear it for the first time. Witnessing is a demonstration of God's grace, lived out in our everyday routines. Richard Gardner, in *Matthew,* from the Believers Church Bible Commentary, points to the blameless lives of the sixteenth-century Anabaptists and their "silent witness" that thoroughly impressed their critics. "They were committed to living out the principles of the gospel in everyday life, and it showed." Gardner quoted a Catholic theologian of that day, Franz Agricola: "Among the existing heretical sects there is none which in appearance leads a more modest, better, or more pious life than the Anabaptists. As concerns their outward public life they are irreproachable. No lying, deception, swearing, strife, harsh language, no intemperate eating and drinking, no outward personal display, is found or discernable among them, but humility, patience, uprightness, neatness, honesty, temperance, straightforwardness in such measure that one would suppose that they have the Holy Spirit of God." What a witness!

The Personal Connection

Paul concluded his letter by telling the Colossians of his co-workers' comings and goings. He thereby helped them understand how connections with one another also serve as a form of witness. As Paul revealed the whereabouts of Tychicus, Onesimus, Aristarchus, Mark, Barnabas, and Jesus called Justus, and as he brought greetings to others, he helped the Colossians feel their unity with Christians in other places. Today, as we provide personal and financial resources to ministries around the world, we enable the kind of connection Paul encouraged in the early church. As we gather to pray for different ministries, we continue to support the worldwide ministry begun by the earliest apostles.

Paul closed with a personal admonition to Archippus from which we, too, can benefit. "See that you complete the task that you have received in the LORD" (4:17). There is always more ministry for the church to carry out, for example, the problems faced by congregations throughout the United States that find themselves surrounded by dangers such as drug trafficking and other violence. I am always impressed and inspired by congregations that mobilize groups of men and women to go out night after and night and place themselves in the streets. The Christians are living witnesses as they patrol their neighborhoods, witnesses to God's desire that evil and destruction have no more influence in these communities than does the church of Jesus Christ.

The work of witness is not yet complete, and will not be, until Christ returns for his people. What do we do in the meantime? We pray for one another. In this way we demonstrate our connection to every other believer in the whole world. With joy Paul prayed for the church in all the places where it was growing, or suffering, or even rebelling and becoming complacent. He taught that prayer is an important ministry for believers because it does, indeed, change things. Prayer is absolutely crucial for a good and healthy witness.

Discussion and Action

1. What are your most deeply held beliefs, the things about which you feel most passionate?

2. One aspect of the "mystery of Christ" is that it broke down the barrier between Jew and Gentile, from the beginning of the church. What are some of the other barriers in the church and society that need breaking down? How can the message of Christ be applied in practical ways to these barriers?
3. How have you felt unity with Christians around the world? In what ways can this global connection be encouraged and upheld in a congregation?
4. What do you think Paul meant by "making the most of the time" in 4:5? In what ways have you been able to carry out this command? In what ways has your congregation been able to do so?
5. Take an index card and pencil. On one side of the card, write an example of "salty speech" (4:6) that you have heard among Christians (something encouraging, conveying a positive witness). On the other side, jot down an example of "peppery speech" that can occur in church circles (something discouraging or hurtful). Read examples aloud and tell how—as appropriate, without naming names—one of the kinds of speech has affected you.
6. Richard Gardner, in the Believers Church Bible Commentary on Matthew, writes of sixteenth-century forebears of Mennonites and Brethren: "The Anabaptists were intensely missionary. They also were uniquely first-generation believers. Faith determined insiders and outsiders, not ethnic or institutional factors. Although they commissioned traveling missionaries, the movement spread largely because all members were internally motivated to share and spread the faith."

   If there are any first-generation believers in your group, ask them to share about what kind of witness brought them to Christ. Discuss the benefits and possible drawbacks of coming from a Christian family of several generations.
7. Have you sensed that non-Christian neighbors or co-workers view the church as composed of the "righteous elite"? In what practical ways could you help non-Christians see that the church is more like a hospital for sinners than a hotel for saints?

10

A Story of Transformation

Philemon

Paul wrote the most personal of his letters as he urged his friend and brother Philemon to accept his runaway slave, Onesimus, as a brother in Christ. The apostle made it clear that spiritual freedom in Christ has implications for human liberation in society.

Personal Preparation

1. Read through the letter to Philemon three times, in three separate sittings. Each time, read it from a different point of view: that of Paul, Onesimus, and Philemon. Later, consider with whom you most identified. Why?
2. Recall a situation in which you had a right to do something in a relationship but willingly chose to forego that right. How difficult was it for you to give up your power or authority? What difference did it make in the relationship?
3. Can you think of anyone who might benefit from your advocacy in the days ahead? Spend some moments reflecting silently about this. Who comes to mind? Who needs your help, support, or encouragement this week? Would a letter of recommendation help?

Understanding

When have you been in a fix that you could not handle by yourself? Did you have a friend or relative that took up your cause and bailed you out? If you have ever had that experience of being helped, then you can relate to the book of Philemon—at least if you read it from the perspective of the runaway slave. Onesimus had a big problem; he was returning from Rome with his hat in his hand. His Colossian master had every legal right to punish the young man (think of the lost hours of work!). Or the master could accept him as a new Christian brother. The words of Onesimus's friend and advocate Paul would make all the difference.

Tradition tells us that Philemon was written by Paul in Rome and sent to Colossae around 63 A.D. Likely it was carried in the hands of Onesimus. Before Paul wrote to his friend Philemon, he apparently converted Onesimus to Christianity. This short, persuasive correspondence focuses on the reunion of slave and owner, particularly the possibility that it will be a reunion of transformed relationship. It was Paul's great hope that Philemon would view Onesimus no longer as an owned commodity, but as a beloved brother. Thus, as Paul wrote to Philemon, he was perfectly clear about what he wanted. He sent back a slave whom he himself had come to think of as a helper and brother.

A Poignant Story for Three Men

There is interpersonal drama and poignancy here. More was at stake, however, than whether the three men would come to terms. Also at issue was how the church would change social relationships in the coming centuries. Paul did not question the legality of slavery, but he did expect Philemon to do a radical thing. Onesimus, whose name is translated as "useful," *could not* be useful in the proclamation of the gospel if he was thought of as mere property. As Christians, Onesimus and Philemon were more like brothers than slave and master. A family member could not be owned by another family member without calling into question the integrity of the household of the church. In Paul's day, this was a revolutionary idea.

Today we question why Paul did not speak out more directly against slavery as the sin that it is. In this regard, scholar F. F. Bruce comments: "What this letter does is to *bring us into an atmosphere* in which the institution [of slavery] could only wilt and die. . . . Formal emancipation would be but a matter of expediency, the technical confirmation of the new relationship that had already come into being." So Paul's strategy is clear. He did not order Philemon to free Onesimus. Instead, he appealed to the "atmosphere"—the radical new context of Christian relating.

First, Paul appealed to Christian love. Paul made a deliberate decision not to use his pastoral authority to command Philemon to free

Onesimus. He wrote, "I would rather appeal to you on the basis of love" (9). Both coercion and persuasion can be effective motivators in human behavior, but one appeals primarily to fear, the other to our sense of wanting to do what we believe to be right because we have been convinced there is some benefit to us and to others. Of course, that also can be true of behavior that is forced, yet the benefit of coercion is that mostly we have acted to avoid our own pain.

When we act on the basis of love, we internalize in a positive way the value of the change we are making. Paul helps us remember that, even though we may rightfully command what we want, it is much more life-giving to seek what we want and need by sharing in the love of God. If Paul had commanded the liberation of Onesimus, Philemon might have received him back, but also he might have taken advantage of all of the legal remedies for dealing with escaped and returned slaves. Such remedies might have included a severe beating and possibly death for the slave.

Second, Paul appealed to consent and partnership. "I preferred to do nothing without your consent. . . . If you consider me your partner" (14, 17). Paul knew that if Philemon welcomed Onesimus back, he would do so only because he believed in his heart that it was the right thing to do. Paul seemed to be urging Philemon to a "win-win" situation, calling on his old friend to be reconciled to Onesimus out of a sense of mutuality and partnership. Paul wanted Philemon to receive the runaway slave into his home as a fellow pilgrim with Christ.

Third, Paul appealed to mutual accountability. These three men were all accountable to one another, yet Paul turned the typical appeal ("Hey, you are *supposed* to do this!") upside down by referring to his own accountability in a humble offer to make restitution. "Charge that to my account. . . . I will repay it" (18-19). Paul was a spiritual mentor to both men, and all three of them belonged to Christ. They were all "Onesimus," in that they were all useful to each other. Each one, in his own way, ought to have been responsible, liable, and available to the others. Of course, it is disturbing that two men apparently would decide the fate of the third. In fact, they all would be profoundly affected by the decision made by Philemon, as would the whole church.

An Unfinished Story for All of Us

The transformation of these three men began when they became Christians. The next step in their transformation came as Philemon decided how Onesimus would be received back into his household. Would he be welcome as a brother in the Lord, or merely as a returned fugitive?

We are left with an unfinished story. We do not know for certain what finally happened. As he signed his letter, Paul was still in prison writing to churches and individuals, doing the good work of spreading the gospel of the risen Christ. Philemon was at home in Colossae, and Onesimus was still a slave. But Paul was confident that Philemon would do the right thing. Some scholars believe that Onesimus eventually became one of the leaders of the church, perhaps even a bishop (see Col. 4:9), but this point is not certain. The story of the lives of the three men is not unlike the story of our own lives—the end is not yet resolved. God's grace still works in us for transformation.

Of course, we have friends and advocates in our lives, people who pray for us and see us through the hard times. Sometimes we do not even know who they are because they do their loving work behind the scenes. The congregation I now serve was without a pastor for fifteen months. I had been without an installed position for twelve months. On the day the congregation voted to call me as their pastor, a woman hugged me warmly and said, "I've been praying for you for over a year—and I didn't even know who you were."

That woman was a liberator for me. As we have studied these three prison epistles of Paul, we have been reminded that we must continue to live out our freedom in Christ and spread the liberating message of the gospel. Keeping our eyes on the prize of perfect freedom in Christ, we may face real or metaphorical prisons daily. Out of those myriad forms of bondage, we have the freedom to proclaim our faith in a way that helps to change the world.

That freedom can never be taken away. I recall the experience of a modern-era prisoner, Victor Frankl, who suffered in the Nazi concentration camps of World War II. His father, mother, brother, and wife all died in the camps, leaving only him and a sister as survivors. Virtually everything was taken from him, yet in his book, *Man's Search for Meaning,* he wrote: "We who lived in concentration camps can remember the men who walked through the huts comforting others, giving away their last piece of bread. They may have been few in number, but they offer sufficient proof that everything can be taken from a [person] but one thing: the last of the human freedoms—*to choose one's attitude in any given set of circumstances.*" Ultimately, it was not Philemon who decided Onesimus's fate; it was Onesimus himself. So it is with all of us. In fellowship with our Lord, we make the choices that determine the quality of our discipleship, no matter what the circumstances.

Recall that as Paul ended his letter to the Colossians, he asked his readers to realize that he did not enjoy his loss of physical freedom. "Remember my chains," he wrote. As we remember people around the world who are prisoners of conscience and people who are prisoners of their own fear and ignorance, let us join with Paul in living out a strong faith and great hope: that the liberating grace of Christ sets us free.

Discussion and Action

1. The book of Philemon has been called the magna carta of human dignity. What evidence do you find in this letter that supports such a title? How would you compare the way slavery is dealt with in Philemon and Colossians?
2. How do the roles of Christian brother and sister transcend other life roles that people play? Relate your response to the themes you find in the book of Philemon.
3. In a sense, Paul had to choose between being authoritarian and being assertive with Philemon. Compare and contrast the two approaches. In what ways do you see these two approaches at work in your family, neighborhood, or work place? How are they present in your church family?
4. From our perspective, we might say that Paul exhibited a kind of incrementalism in his approach to the slavery issue. In other words, he was willing to work with small gains in the present, hoping to achieve larger gains in the future. How do you feel about that? Do you believe we should strive for small, step-by-step changes in our imperfect world, or should we settle only for a complete change in order to forcefully create the perfect situation? Can you give a practical example of such a situation from your own experience?
5. Victor Frankl spoke of our ultimate ability to choose our attitude in every situation. Do you agree with his statement? How would you apply this principle to the problem of prejudice in our society? For example, how do you balance the legitimate focus on blame for the slavery in our history and the responsibility to choose a positive attitude about the future?

6. Samuel Rutherford, a seventeenth-century Scottish reformer, headed his letters from prison: "Christ's Palace, Aberdeen." He proclaimed that "every stone in the wall shone like a ruby." Have you ever been able to take such a positive attitude to a "personal prison" because of your relationship to Christ? Can you talk with the group about this experience?
7. Bring your study unit to a close by considering these questions: What have you learned about the Apostle Paul during these ten weeks? What have you learned about yourselves? In what ways have you been challenged to grow? How have you been called to action? What questions have been raised in your minds? What are your new perspectives on personal imprisonment and freedom?

Suggestions for Sharing and Prayer

This material is designed for covenant groups that spend one hour sharing and praying together, followed by one hour of Bible study. The suggestions given here will help relate the group's sharing and praying to its study of *Paul's Prison Letters*. You will find session-by-session ideas as well as ideas that carry through all ten meetings. General resources for sharing and prayer follow. These ideas are written by Mary Jessup and June Gibble. Use the ideas you find most helpful, and bring your own creative ideas to your group.

Four related themes run through these materials and will become part of your group life: (1) letters of encouragement, thanksgiving, and support, which you will be encouraged to write each week; (2) Christ hymns or affirmations that you will discover in scripture, hymns, affirmations of faith, and your own experience in the form of words and phrases that help you understand Jesus Christ; (3) Christ-likeness or learning to live in Christ's new way, which you are encouraged to covenant to practice during this study through spiritual exercises and disciplines; (4) freedom in Christ, freedom from bondage and imprisonment, and freedom to a new life, which you will find growing out of scripture, hymns, and action projects related to bondage and freedom.

We have suggested a special note-writing project for all group members. Each person writes a note of appreciation, thanks, support, or encouragement for all other group members each week, holding these notes until the last session. Then all the notes will be handed out to be opened and read as part of the group's closure.

1. Persisting, Though Opposed

- ❑ Create an atmosphere for your group life and worship. Before your first meeting, invite group members to bring a symbol of their faith that will become part of the week's worship center. First, place a large, unusual candle on a small table or worship center, and light it. Then create your worship center as each person places her or his faith symbol on the worship center and explains the symbol's meaning.

- ❑ Decide how you will create this worship center each time you meet. Plan to bring something that symbolizes the theme of each session. For session 2, for example, bring something that calls you to have the mind of Christ. Suggestions are given at the beginning of each session. You might want to bring back the same symbols each week, but arrange them differently.
- ❑ Note the joy and thanksgiving in Paul's letter, even though he was imprisoned. Talk about times of difficulty that intimately influenced your lives for the better. How were you able to find joy or thanksgiving in the midst of difficulty?
- ❑ Focus on these words in Paul's prayer, sent to the church at Philippi: "That the one who began a good work among you will bring it to completion by the day of Jesus Christ" (Phil. 1:6). Paul began the work in Philippi, but the task of carrying on the ministry soon fell to others. On a large piece of newsprint, make a timeline for your congregation noting dates of events, people who started significant work, and others who carried it on.
- ❑ Plan a letterwriting action as part of each meeting. This week, note the affection and gratitude Paul expressed for the Philippian church. Write letters or notes to congregations for which you feel affection and gratitude. Mail your letters this week.
- ❑ Sing a chorus about joy in the faith, such as "Joy is flowing like a river" or "I've got joy, joy, joy, joy down in my heart." Follow the song by sentence prayers such as, "Thank you, God, for this joy in my life" (with each person naming a special joy).
- ❑ Conclude each sharing and prayer time with a Philippians blessing or benediction, for example, "Rejoice in the LORD always; again I will say, Rejoice" (Phil. 4:4). You may want to sing the musical form of this blessing:

  Rejoice in the Lord always, and again I say rejoice.
  Rejoice in the Lord always, and again I say rejoice.
  Rejoice, rejoice, and again I say rejoice.
  Rejoice, rejoice, and again I say rejoice.

2. Having the Mind of Christ

- ❑ Create a worship center with symbols that represent having the mind of Christ. Read together the words from Philippians 2:5: "Let the same mind be in you that was in Christ Jesus."
- ❑ Talk about a time when you listened deeply to another person and were able to see things from that person's point of view. How did that conversation change your understanding, your attitudes, and your actions?
- ❑ Note Paul's mention of the serious illness of Epaphroditus. Write a get-well note to someone who is ill, and pray for that person during the week.
- ❑ Read Philippians 2:5-11, an early Christian hymn, in several translations. Begin to memorize this hymn about Christ, using your favorite translation. Speak it once a day and share it during a later group session. Consider paraphrasing this Christ hymn, putting it into your own words. You may want to memorize your own paraphrased version.
- ❑ Look at the words of a recent hymn based on Philippians 2:5-11: "Christ, who is in the form of God" (see General Sharing and Prayer Resources). Note how closely these words parallel the Christ hymn. Imagine early Christians singing this hymn. You may want to learn the hymn and sing it together.
- ❑ Respond to the call to be a servant, like Christ, reading the words of the hymn, "Will you let me be your servant." Have different people read the different stanzas, with all joining on the last one. If yours is a singing group, sing this hymn.
- ❑ Make a list of people who embody for you the words, "children of God . . . you shine like stars in the world" (Phil. 2:15). Have group members write these names on a large poster board, telling why they include each name. Then pray prayers of thanksgiving for each person listed, such as, "God, we thank you for__________, who shines like a star in this world." Close with a group "Amen."

3. A Warning . . . and a Prize

- ❑ Bring to your worship center symbols that speak of your relationship to Jesus Christ. Refer to these scripture passages: "I want to know Christ" (Phil. 3:10) and "Christ Jesus has made me his own" (Phil. 3:12). Again share the meaning of each symbol.
- ❑ Have each person draw a line representing the time span of his or her life. Mark two high points and two low points on the line. Invite people to think about their relationships with God and with Jesus at these high and low points. Share these reflections with the group.
- ❑ Talk about times you have needed to make a break with the past and move on to something new. What helps you let go of the past and find the value in the new?
- ❑ Name some athletes who have been an inspiration to you. What special qualities do you admire in them? How are these qualities helpful in the Christian walk of faith?
- ❑ Talk about committing to a spiritual exercise program, even as athletes commit to regular exercise. Covenant with each other for a regular spiritual growth exercise such as reading an inspirational book, meditating each day at a regular time, fasting from food or television or something else, writing to prisoners, working for abolition of the death penalty, or participating in a community project. Perhaps two or three people in the group will choose one exercise; maybe the whole group will do the same one. Make your commitments to God and to each other. Decide how you will share progress reports with each other.
- ❑ Pray together using the words of the hymn, "If all you want, Lord." First read the words, noting the humor in being willing to give something, but not everything! Pray the words silently, then read or sing this hymn as a group prayer and as your commitment to God.

  If all you want, Lord, is my heart,
my heart is yours alone—
providing I may set apart
my mind to be my own.

  If all you want, Lord, is my mind,
my mind belongs to you,
but let my heart remain inclined
to do what it would do.

If heart and mind would both suffice,
while I kept strength and soul,
at least I would not sacrifice
completely my control.

But since, O God, you want them all
to shape with your own hand,
I pray for grace to heed your call
to live your first command.

4. Inner Peace . . . Lived Out

- ❑ On the worship center place symbols of inner peace that are important for your faith life. Share something about their meaning.
- ❑ "Rejoice in the LORD always. . . . The LORD is near" (Phil. 4:4-5). When do you rejoice in the Lord? How do you rejoice and know that God is near at all times?
- ❑ Give personal examples of the difference you have found between "the pursuit of happiness," about which we hear so much in our culture, and the experience of joy.
- ❑ Write notes thanking someone for financial, emotional, or spiritual support, even as Paul wrote his thanks to the Philippian congregation for its support.
- ❑ Talk about how your spiritual growth commitment is progressing. Offer support and encouragement to each other. Recommit as a group to continue this discipline through the next six weeks.
- ❑ Meditate on the words found in Philippians 4:8. First, read them together slowly and reflectively. Then meditate on each phrase, as one person reads the text aloud phrase by phrase, pausing for silence after these key words: *beloved, true, honorable, just, pure, pleasing, commendable, excellence, praise, things*. After a period of silence, again read the verse together.
- ❑ Sing favorite hymns about inner peace. Have each person name a favorite hymn about peace and then sit in the middle of the group to listen while the group sings his or her hymn. Do this for all group members. Use Philippians 4:7 as your benediction.

5. Treasure Here!

- ❑ Bring to the worship center items that symbolize Christ and his reconciliation (Col. 1:20).
- ❑ Note that Paul again prayed for people he loved. Talk about the people you know are remembering you in prayer. Is there anyone who has "not ceased praying for you," as Paul wrote (Col. 1:9)? How does it feel to know that you are being held up to God in prayer?
- ❑ Write notes to the youth in your congregation, recognizing their faith in Christ Jesus and encouraging them to continue to "grow in the knowledge of God" (Col. 1:10). Hand deliver or mail these notes.
- ❑ Read the Christ-hymn in Colossians 1:15-20. Compare this hymn to the one in Philippians 2:5-11. How are they alike? Where do they differ? List all the names or phrases in these two texts that tell who Jesus is. Add other words that are important to your understanding and expression of who Jesus is. Also name favorite hymns whose words or phrases help you understand better the fullness of Jesus Christ. Sing some of these hymns.
- ❑ Talk about these two Christ-hymns as early Christian affirmations of faith. What faith affirmations are part of your faith tradition? Some Christians use the Apostles' Creed or the Nicene Creed; others use their own denomination's affirmation of faith. How are such affirmations important for your faith?
- ❑ Pray sentence prayers of thanksgiving, each person praying for the person on her or his right. After each prayer, all join in the unison declaration from Colossians 1:27: "Christ in you, ________, the hope of glory."

6. Warning: Hazardous to Your (Spiritual) Health!

- ❑ Bring to your worship center reminders of a person who helped you to be "rooted and built up" in Christ (Col. 2:7). Briefly share the person's name and how he or she gave you that rootedness.
- ❑ Write a note of thanks to someone who helped you to be rooted in the faith or who helped you to grow into deeper understanding as you rethought a belief or position.

- ❑ Report about the spiritual exercises or disciplines that you have been doing. How are they helping you to "continue to live your lives" in Christ (Col. 2:6)? What kind of encouragement or accountability from each other do you want or need?
- ❑ Learn a hymn about new life and freedom in Christ: "Lift every voice and sing." Read the words, or listen as one person reads them. Play the hymn on a piano or other instrument. Listen as a musician sings it for you, then sing along. This hymn has been called the African American national anthem. Can you see why? How does it speak to your need for freedom and new life?
- ❑ Remember that Martin Luther, when experiencing despair, found comfort by touching his forehead and saying, "I am baptized." Remembering our own baptism can help us keep centered in the faith during times of despair or struggle. Share memories of your baptism. Close the sharing by touching your forehead and saying, "I am baptized." When all have finished, join together in saying, "We remember our baptism and we are thankful."
- ❑ Close by praying the prayer of St. Richard of Chichester, or singing the hymn version:

  Day by day, dear Lord,
  of thee, three things I pray:
  to see thee more clearly,
  love thee more dearly,
  follow thee more nearly,
  day by day.

7. Put On Those Heavenly Clothes

- ❑ Create your worship center with symbols that speak of love, each person explaining the meaning of his or her symbol. Sing together, as the Colossians were instructed, "with gratitude in your hearts . . . psalms, hymns, and spiritual songs to God" (Col. 3:16).
- ❑ Think about words and actions that hurt or harm things that you or others have used (the old ways or "old clothes"). Write these things on note cards, then tear the cards into pieces and burn them or put them in a wastebasket.
- ❑ Talk about words and actions that have helped and healed—the "new clothes" of life in Christ. Give a blessing to each other by

one person standing and laying hands on the other and praying, "Dear God, bless ________ (give a name and request for blessing). Amen." Change places and give the second blessing.

- ❑ Write a note to one person whose life has blessed yours, or to a person who gave you a special blessing at a significant time.
- ❑ Sing the chorus, "Standin' in the need of prayer." Then pray in unison this confession of sin from *The Book of Common Prayer:*

  Most merciful God,
  we confess that we have sinned against you
  in thought, word, and deed,
  by what we have done,
  and by what we have left undone.
  We have not loved you with our whole heart;
  we have not loved our neighbors as ourselves.
  We are truly sorry and we humbly repent.
  For the sake of your son Jesus Christ,
  have mercy on us and forgive us;
  that we may delight in your will,
  and walk in your ways,
  to the glory of your name. Amen.

- ❑ Read together the assurance of pardon found in 1 John 1:9—"If we confess our sins, he who is faithful and just will forgive us our sins and cleanse us from all unrighteousness." Thanks be to God!
- ❑ Pray the well-known prayer hymn by John Greenleaf Whittier: "Dear Lord and Father of Mankind" (see General Sharing and Prayer Resources). You may pray the words together, sing the hymn as a prayer, or listen in silent prayer as one person reads or sings the hymn.
- ❑ Close with a blessing from Numbers 6:24-26, with one person reading the benediction one phrase at a time and the group repeating it:

  The LORD bless you and keep you;
  the LORD make his face to shine upon you,
  and be gracious to you;
  the LORD lift up his countenance upon you,
  and give you peace. Amen.

8. Family Life Yesterday and Today

- ❑ Create your worship center by bringing symbols from memorable times in the lives of your families. Talk about the meaning of those times. Then read together this paraphrase of Psalm 78:3-7 (have it printed in large letters on a bright-colored board and place it as part of your worship center):

  We will speak of things we have heard and known,
  things our ancestors have told us.
  We will not hide these things from our children;
  but we will tell the coming generation of your glorious deeds, O God,
  and the wonders you have done. . . .
  And they will teach their children,
  so that the next generation might know them,
  and tell their children to set their hope in God.

- ❑ Sing choruses you learned as children in your families or in Sunday school. Let group members begin a chorus and all join in.
- ❑ Share ways in which your families have recently celebrated a season of the Christian year such as Advent, Christmas, Lent, Easter, Pentecost. How have the celebrations strengthened your families and your faith?
- ❑ Write note cards to send or hand-deliver to some of the families in your congregation. Express support and encouragement where you know it is needed.
- ❑ Remember bedtime prayers and rituals in your families. Think about families around the world. What must bedtime be like where war is raging or disease and famine are rampant? Pray now for the world's families and children.
- ❑ Write together a litany or a prayer for today's families: your own, those in your congregation, and families around the world. Pray this together as your closing.

9. Keep On Witnessing

- ❑ Bring things to your prayer center that aid you in your prayer lives. Talk about your symbols and also tell when prayer has changed you or changed something in your lives.

- ❑ Write notes or letters to friends who were once part of your congregation and have now moved away. Send greetings and express thanks for the unity you have in Christ. You may want to write these as a group project.
- ❑ Name some ministries that are worthy of your personal and financial support. Pray for these local and global ministries and the people they touch.
- ❑ Note Paul's statement, "See that you complete the task that you have received in the LORD (Col. 4:17). Name people whose lives have shown that they have completed their tasks. Talk about their lives, tell how they witnessed to you, and thank God for their witness.
- ❑ Find hymns in your hymnal about being a witness for Christ and witnessing to your faith. Find some that are written as prayers. One example is "Guide My Feet." Together read these words as your prayer. Learn to sing the hymn as a prayer also.

10. A Story of Transformation

- ❑ Create your prayer place with symbols of newfound freedom. Invite each person to talk about a time they were in bondage or felt imprisoned and then were freed.
- ❑ Talk about experiences of transformation in your lives, families, church, and faith journeys.
- ❑ Reflect quietly on difficult times in a relationship, when you needed to go to a third person for help in strengthening that relationship. Then talk in general about how a third person, such as Paul in this text, can bring new light on relationship problems.
- ❑ Report to the group about how you have experienced your commitment to a spiritual exercise or discipline. Give support to those who want to continue their commitments. Give thanks to God for spiritual growth you have experienced. Sing "Guide my feet" as your prayer for God's continued presence.
- ❑ Close by giving notes of thanksgiving, support, appreciation, and encouragement to each member of the group. These will have been written, one per week, during your ten weeks together. Allow time for the giving and the reading of these notes. Close by singing "Blest be the tie that binds" (see General Sharing and Prayer Resources).

General Sharing and Prayer Resources

An Affirmation of Faith Used by the Church of the Brethren

Leader: He was the Son of God.
All: He was the Son of Man.
Leader: He came down from heaven.
All: He was born in a stable.
Leader: Kings came to his cradle.
All: His first home was a cave.
Leader: He was born to be a king.
All: He was a child of Mary.
Leader: He was the greatest among rulers.
All: He was the least among servants.
Leader: He was loved and honored.
All: He was despised and rejected.
Leader: He was gentle and loving.
All: He made many enemies.
Leader: He counseled perfection.
All: He was a friend of sinners.
Leader: He was a joyful companion.
All: He was a man of sorrows.
Leader: He said, 'Rejoice.'
All: He said, 'Repent.'
Leader: 'Love God with all your heart.'
All: 'Love your neighbor as yourself.'
Leader: 'Don't be anxious.'
All: 'Count the cost.'
Leader: 'Deny yourself.'
All: 'Ask and receive.'
Leader: In him was life.
All: He died on a cross.
Leader: He was a historic person.
All: He lives today.
Leader: He was Jesus of Nazareth.
All: He is Christ the Lord.

An Affirmation of Faith Used by the Christian Church (Disciples of Christ)

As members of the Christian Church,
We confess that Jesus is the Christ,
the Son of the living God,
and proclaim him Lord and Savior of the world.
In Christ's name and by his grace
we accept our mission of witness
and service to all people.
We rejoice in God,
maker of heaven and earth,
and in the covenant of love that
binds us to God and one another.
Through baptism into Christ
we enter into newness of life
and are made one with the whole people of God.
In the communion of the Holy Spirit
we are joined together in discipleship
and in obedience to Christ.
At the table of the Lord
we celebrate with thanksgiving
the saving acts and presence of Christ.
Within the universal church
we receive the gift of ministry
and the light of scripture.
In the bonds of Christian faith
we yield ourselves to God
that we many serve the One
whose kingdom has no end.
Blessing, glory, and honor
be to God forever. Amen.

A Prayer Hymn: "Dear Lord and Father of Mankind"

Dear Lord and Father of mankind, forgive our foolish ways.
Reclothe us in our rightful mind,
in purer lives thy service find,
in deeper rev'rence praise.

In simple trust like theirs who heard, beside the Syrian sea,
the gracious calling of the Lord,
let us, like them, without a word
rise up and follow thee.

O Sabbath rest by Galilee! O calm of hills above,
where Jesus knelt to share with thee
the silence of eternity,
interpreted by love;

drop thy still dews of quietness, 'til all our strivings cease.
Take from our souls the strain and stress,
and let our ordered lives confess
the beauty of thy peace.

Breathe through the heats of our desire thy coolness and thy balm.
Let sense be dumb, let flesh retire,
speak through the earthquake, wind, and fire,
O still small voice of calm!

—John Greenleaf Whittier, 1872

Christ, who is in the form of God

Text: Based on Philippians 2:6 11.
Music: Orlando Gibbons, 1623

Bless'd be the tie that binds

Text: John Fawcett, 1782
Music: Johann G. Nageli. Adapted by Lowell Mason, 1845

My life flows on

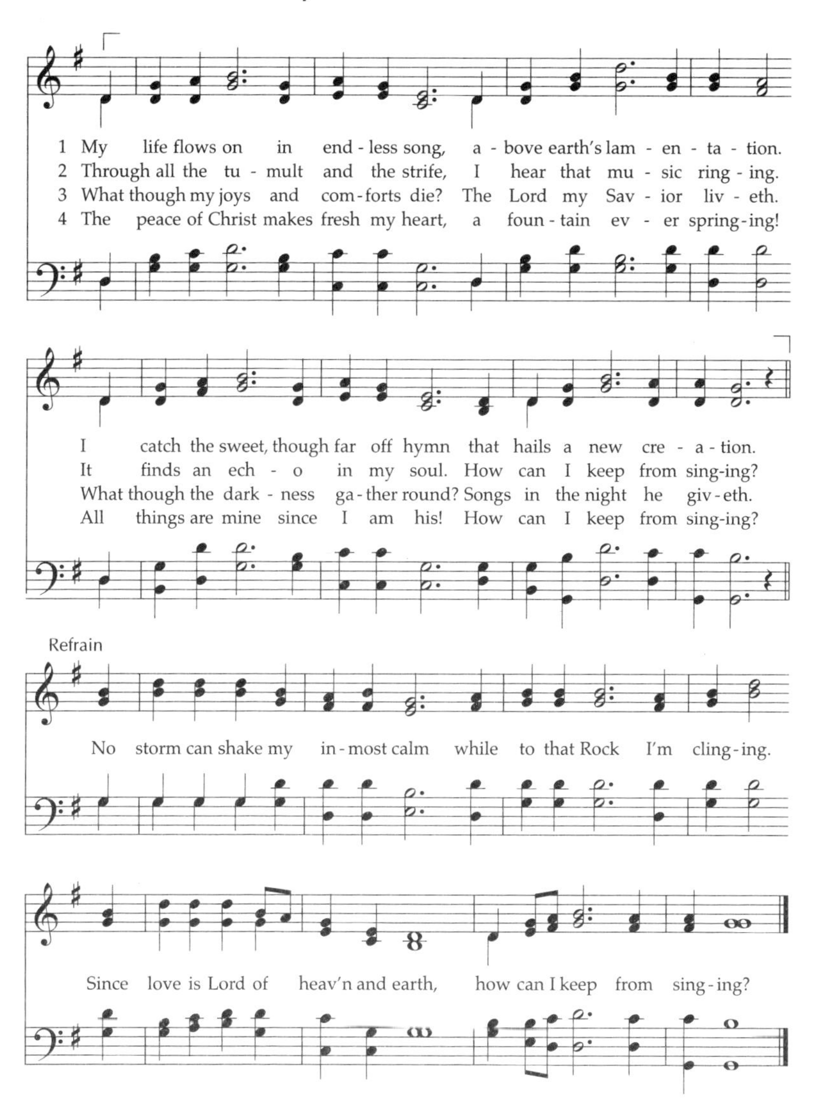

Text and Music: Robert Lowry, 1869, alt.

Awake, my soul

Text: Philip Doddridge, 1755
Music: George F. Handel, 1728. Adapted 1812